THE
FINANCIAL
HOUSE

A CUSTOM-DESIGNED FINANCIAL PLAN TO HELP
YOU BUILD YOUR DREAM RETIREMENT

ERIC L. SCOTT,
PAUL SCOTT &
KATIE PROSSER

Katie Prosser
555 S. Bluff St. Ste. 302
St. George, UT 84770
www.ericscottfinancial.com
info@ericscottfinancial.com
435.773.9444

The Financial House/Eric L. Scott, Paul Scott & Katie Prosser.
—1st Edition

ISBN: 9798863171890

IMPORTANT DISCLOSURES

The content contained in this book is believed to be factual and up to date, as of the time of its publication, but we do not guarantee its accuracy and it should not be regarded as a complete analysis of the subjects discussed.

The information provided herein is intended to be educational in nature and is not intended to be a recommendation for any specific investment or insurance product, strategy, feature or any action at all and is not endorsed or affiliated with the Social Security Administration or any government agency. Accordingly, it should not be construed by any consumer and/or prospective client as solicitation to effect, or attempt to effect transactions in securities, or the rendering of personalized investment or insurance advice for compensation.

Any references to tax or legal subject matter is strictly for informational purposes only. No person associated with Eric Scott Financial is a licensed tax professional or attorney and nothing in this book should be construed as tax or legal advice.

The main characters are fictional, and the scenarios discussed are not real and intended for illustrative purposes only.

This book may contain forward-looking statements based on hypothetical assumptions, estimates, outlook, and other judgments made in light of information available at the time this book was written and involve both known and unknown risks and uncertainties. Accordingly, plans, goals, and other statements may not be realized as described and actual financial results, success/failure or may differ materially from those presented herein.

Prior to making any investment, insurance or financial decisions, an investor should seek individualized advice from a licensed financial, legal or tax professional that takes into account all of the particular facts and circumstances of an investor's own situation.

Eric L. Scott and Eric Scott Financial, LLC offer investment advisory services through APO Financial Services, LLC, an investment adviser registered with the Securities and Exchange Commission. Registration with the SEC should not be construed to imply that the SEC has approved or endorsed qualifications, or the services offered, or that its personnel possess a particular level of skill, expertise or training.

Additional information pertaining to APO's registration status, its business operations, services and fees, its current written disclosure statement and its investment advisor representatives is available on the SEC's Investment Adviser public website at https://www.adviserinfo.sec.gov.

Insurance and fixed annuity products are offered through Scott Insurance Inc, Asset Protect One, Inc, and/or APO Financial Services, Inc for which licensed insurance producers receive commission when products are sold.

Dedicated to our family:
Sherri, Ryan, Mike,
Lexi, Calvin, Oriana, and Addison

Special thanks:
Lola Dunn, Editor

Karl Thurman, Insurance Consultant
Key City Insurance (KeyCityInsurance.com)

Michael Dunn, Estate Attorney Consultant
Dunn Law Firm (DunnFirm.com)

Ryan Long, Gold & Silver Consultant
National Gold Consultants
(NationalGoldConsultants.com)

TABLE OF CONTENTS

A SHIFT IN PERSPECTIVE

Chapter One

THE BARBECUE

The cooking grate sizzled as Tom placed another ribeye on the grill. He wiped his forehead with his sleeve and picked up the near-by glass of lemonade.

"I appreciate you coming out, Rob," he said to the man standing beside him, eagerly watching the meat cook.

"Not every day a man retires, Tom. We're happy to be here," Robert replied, lifting his own glass of lemonade in a playful toast. They clinked their glasses together. "Besides, if I'm being honest, you grill a better steak than I do."

Tom laughed as he flipped one of the steaks.

"Just the right shade of reddish brown, and look at those grill marks," Robert said, shaking his head. "Mmm, mm, mm."

"So, how about you, Robert?" Tom asked his neighbor. "When will we be invited to your retirement party?"

Robert chuckled half-heartedly, running his hand through his thinning hair. "I don't know. Probably not for a few more years, at least."

"Really?" Tom asked, surprised. He grabbed one of the steaks with his tongs and placed it on the warming plate. "Last time we spoke, it sounded like you and Jenny were ready to leave the workforce behind."

"Oh, we're plenty ready," Robert said, laughing. "I'm just not sure we can afford to right now." He took another sip of lemonade, thoughtfully. "Honestly, I'm not sure when that time will come. With everything I've seen in the economy the past few years, the way the market's been going up and down …" he trailed off a bit. "I think I'm just concerned that we don't have enough money to last the rest of our lives."

Tom nodded. "Sounds like you need to switch your perspective. Lisa and I were worried about the same things. We made and remade our retirement plan about a dozen times, but it was so hard to pull the trigger."

"That's where we are right now, Jen and I," Robert said, shaking his head.

Tom transferred another steak from the grill to the warming plate. "Well, what's holding you back?" he asked.

"I'd like to think we have enough money to give us a comfortable retirement," Robert said, "but I've lost big money in the market before. I mean, you remember '08. What happens to our retirement if something like that happens again?"

*****

Inside, Jennifer stood in the kitchen chopping some romaine lettuce for the salad, while Lisa sliced carrots and celery for dipping.

"I thought you had a solid savings plan," Lisa said, cutting away the leaves from the celery stalks. "So, what's the trouble?"

"For me, it's a question of health care," Jenny answered. "What if there's an accident? I mean, if one of us needs extra care or an extended hospital stay, our retirement savings could go down the drain like that," she said, snapping her fingers.

Lisa smiled sympathetically. "I know what you mean."

"Poor health runs in my family," Jenny said, slicing some watermelon into small cubes to add to the salad. "Both my parents needed a lot of care as they aged, which they continued to need until they passed away. The extra financial burden was overwhelming. My siblings and I even had to pitch in to cover expenses toward the end. Long story short, their money ran dry paying for healthcare. I just don't want Rob to be left with debt if something happens to me."

"You wouldn't want the reverse situation either," Lisa added.

"There's just something so comforting about those paychecks arriving in our bank account every couple of weeks," Jenny said, smiling and shaking her head. "I know we're fine, but I guess we're just nervous to take that next step. A lot of 'what ifs' are floating around in my head right now."

"I understand completely," Lisa agreed as she sprinkled feta cheese over the top of the greens, cucumbers, and watermelon slices they'd prepared.

*****

"I just want to know that she's taken care of should something happen to me," Robert said. "Statistics say men are more likely to die first. I don't want to leave her with nothing if I pass away before she does."

"That makes sense," Tom said. "It's comforting to know that Lisa will be okay when I'm gone and that I'll be okay if she happens to go first. At least, financially, anyway," he added with a small laugh.

"That," Robert replied, pointing at Tom's smile, "right there. That feeling. When you say you *know you'll be okay financially*. How did you get to that point? How are you so sure?"

"Well," Tom said, "between us—"

"We're ready," Lisa interrupted as she and Jenny came out into the backyard, each carrying a tray of delicious-looking sides – the salad, a vegetable tray with dip, and corn on the cob. "How 'bout you fellas? Those steaks done?"

"Just about," Tom said, using the spatula to lift and peek at the bottom of the final sizzling steak.

"Looks good, Lisa," Robert said, crossing the lawn to kiss Jenny on the cheek. "Thanks, hon. You ladies sure worked hard."

"Unlike us," Tom said, winking at his friend, as he approached the table with the tray of steaks. "Hey hon, Rob and I were just talking about something interesting. He was wondering how we were so sure about my decision to retire."

"That's funny," Lisa said, "Jenny and I were having a similar chat."

"Well," Tom said, raising an eyebrow and smirking. "Should we tell them?"

"Tell us what?" Jenny asked wryly. "Tom, did you rob a bank? Is that how you managed it?"

Tom laughed. "No, no. Nothing like that."

"I think they ought to know the whole story, Tom," Lisa said with a knowing look at her husband.

"Please," Robert said. "The suspense is killing me. What's your secret?"

"The secret's not exactly 'what,' but 'who'," Lisa answered, smiling at him.

"Who?"

Tom and Lisa looked at each other and nodded. "The Architect," they said together as if on cue.

Robert and Jenny exchanged confused glances.

"You're downsizing?" Jenny asked, looking at Lisa.

"What?! No!" Lisa replied, shocked.

"Then are you building a vacation house?" Robert asked Tom.

"No," Tom said, laughing as he took another sip of lemonade. He crossed the table to pull out Lisa's chair for her. "We're talking about a Financial Architect."

"Financial Architect?" Robert asked as he followed Tom's lead.

"He helped us build our Financial House," Lisa said, sitting down and giving Jenny's hand a squeeze. "We've never felt so confident about our money in all our lives."

"So, he's an advisor?" Robert asked a bit sardonically. "Because we've already seen our share of brokers and advisors. Most of them try to sell us their company's newest 'sure thing.' I don't know if that's the way we want to go."

"That's right," Jenny added, "they talk about lower fees and better returns, but even if they're right, we've never seen a significant difference. Like Rob said, we've seen all the bells and whistles before."

"Well, you haven't met a guy quite like the Architect— guaranteed," Tom replied. "Rob, this guy's different. He doesn't think in terms of products. He sees your purpose, your dreams, and your life mission. He can help you."

Robert and Jenny exchanged quizzical looks. They had seen so many advisors over the years that this seemed too good to be true. But Tom and Lisa were their close friends. They wouldn't recommend just anyone. Maybe this "Architect" would be different. Robert looked down at his plate, deep in thought.

Sensing Robert's hesitancy, Tom pulled his wallet out and fished through the pockets. "Here," he said, holding a small business card out for his friend.

Robert reached out to take the card, but Tom withdrew his hand and looked very seriously at Robert. "Don't take it unless you mean it. By accepting this card, you're committing to the first step of a journey that will change your life forever."

Robert looked at the card, then up at Tom, a skeptical look on his face. "Is this guy really *that* different?"

"He's that different," Tom said.

"He's the real deal," Lisa agreed.

"Take the card, Rob," Tom said, offering the card again. This time, he allowed Robert to take it.

Robert looked at it curiously. He looked for a number or email address but didn't see either. Only the logo of a small house and the words "The Architect" scrawled in a sophisticated gold font above an unimposing address—123 Retirement Drive.

"There's no contact information here," Robert said, holding the card up to Tom and flipping it back and forth to show him.

"Of course not," Tom said. "You must truly be committed to see the Architect. He won't meet with you until you've truly made up your minds."

"So, how do we get in touch with him?" Robert asked.

"Oh, don't worry, dear," Lisa said. "When you're ready, just go to the address on the card."

Jenny looked at her friend, confused. Lisa only smiled knowingly and patted Jenny's hand.

"We'll definitely hold on to this," Robert said, tucking the card into his wallet for safekeeping. "For now, Tom, it's your retirement party. Let's enjoy this lovely dinner."

"For he's a jolly good fellow," Jenny started to sing. The rest joined in. Tom just shook his head, turning red with embarrassment and raising his hands in protest to no avail.

The barbecue continued well into the night, with the two couples sitting near Tom and Lisa's fire pit sharing stories of bygone days as the flames crackled in the summer evening.

All the while, however, Robert and Jenny thought of the mysterious Architect. Who was he? What could he do for their financial plan that no other advisor had done before?

Was it possible that retirement was on their horizon? Seeing the confidence with which Tom greeted his retirement gave them a glimmer of hope that perhaps great things were just around the corner.

Questions to Consider

1. If you're nearing retirement, what concerns are holding you back?

____

____

____

____

____

____

2. If you're already retired, what major concerns do you have going forward?

____

____

____

____

Chapter Two

THE ARCHITECT

Early the next week, Robert and Jenny parked their car in the parking lot outside the address on the card they had received—123 Retirement Drive.

"Are we *really* sure about this?" Robert asked his wife. "Tom and Lisa were acting so secretive last week when they gave us that card."

"They really seemed adamant about his skills," Jenny said. "I think we have to at least give him a chance. Let's just hope he's as amazing as Tom and Lisa insisted."

Robert nodded resolutely and moved out of the car, walking around to open the door for his wife. They walked across the lot until they stood outside the two great wooden doors of a colonial-looking building, nervously staring at the handles. Something felt different about this whole experience. Something told them opening that door would change things, like throwing a stone into a still lake.

"Well, hi there, folks," a man said, opening the door before they had a chance to turn the knob. "Let me get that door for you two. Come on in. I'm excited to have you both here today. I'm the Architect."

Robert and Jenny exchanged a glance and sized up their mysterious host. He was a sturdy, tall man with salt-and-peppered hair wearing tan dress pants and a cornflower blue button-down without a tie. He had a broad welcoming smile and a recognizable warmth about him.

"You're the Architect?" Jenny asked, shocked.

"Why, of course!" he exclaimed. "Were you expecting someone different?"

"Well, not exactly," Jenny replied, recovering herself, "It's just that our friends Tom and Lisa were so cryptic when they talked about you. I thought you'd be some crazy nut straight out of a novel, like Willy Wonka or someone like that."

"I get that a lot," he replied, shrugging with a sly smile. "I'm actually just your average Joe. It's the work I do that makes me a bit larger than life."

"Now you two," he added, changing the focus, "Mr. and Mrs. Brown, I've been extremely excited to meet the both of you."

"You know who we are?" Robert asked. "We didn't set an appointment or anything. We would have, except there was no number on the card."

"It's Robert and Jennifer, right?" the Architect asked.

Robert nodded. "How did you know?"

"I was informed of your visit," the Architect replied.

"Tom and Lisa must have called you to let you know we'd be coming," Robert reasoned.

"But they didn't know we'd be coming today," Jenny murmured to her husband, a little mystified.

"Well, regardless of the source, I was told you were ready," the Architect said with a nonchalant wave and smirk.

"Mysterious," Robert said. "Still, we are ready."

"Then come on in," the Architect said with a smile, "please, make yourselves at home."

The Architect led them down a short hallway to an office. When he opened the door, however, the room felt less like an office and more like a cozy living room. The room boasted plush furniture, decorative plants, and even a fireplace.

"Please, have a seat," he motioned them toward the couch. They admired the atmosphere in the room as they sat and settled in. Paintings hung on the walls depicting various historical figures, presidents, authors, and actors.

The Architect flipped a switch on the wall, and a fireplace roared to life. Then he sat down in a chair across from the couple and smiled at them.

"I have to say, this all seems a little unorthodox," Jenny said, glancing at the fire, "but our friends Tom and Lisa recommended you very highly, and we trust their judgment."

"Oh yes, Tom and Lisa are great," the Architect replied. "I certainly do things differently. Still, if I conducted business like everyone else, you wouldn't be here, would you?"

"I suppose that's true," Robert replied, nodding.

"I see you're admiring our artwork," the Architect said. "What do you think of the pieces on this wall behind you?"

Robert and Jenny turned around, noticing pictures on the wall of some very unconventional houses. These were homes you'd expect to find in places like Oz or Wonderland, each stranger than the next.

"Would you look at that one?" Jenny asked, nudging her husband.

He shifted his gaze toward hers. "How peculiar!"

"The roof doesn't even cover the house," Robert commented. "It's so small, it only covers a quarter of it."

"And that one's the opposite," Jenny said, pointing at another image. "That roof must be twice the size of the house it sits on. It looks like it could flatten the whole structure at any moment."

"These aren't just any houses," the Architect explained. "These are Financial Houses. Some of my previous clients have come to me with strange financial homes such as these, poorly constructed by no fault of their own. They just took the advice of people who didn't understand the Financial House quite like we do here. Once I finish helping them design their newly customized Financial Houses, they tend to find them much more reasonable. These are the finished Financial Houses they can feel proud of."

The pictures on the walls transformed before the couple's eyes into paintings of beautiful homes. The homes looked so different Jenny and Robert hardly recognized them.

"So, you take the crazy Financial Houses and rebuild them from scratch into something better?" Robert asked.

"Something like that," the Architect replied. "I like to think that I simply collect the existing materials for each house and help my clients redesign their structure to make it more comfortable. When their houses are comfortable, they align with my clients' values and priorities and are more suited to their needs.

"To get started designing *your* Financial House, I'd like to know a little bit more about who you are. Tell me your dreams, your values, your story as it were."

"Well, what do you want to know?" Jenny asked. "There's a lot to tell."

"First, I want you both to close your eyes," he replied. When they had, he continued. "Now, I want you to picture your dream retirement for a moment. What do you see?"

"Golfing," Robert said.

"Maybe you are," Jenny teased, jabbing him playfully with her elbow. "I'm visiting my grandchildren and spoiling them rotten."

"Wonderful," the Architect said, chuckling. "I always believed the best part of being a grandparent is spoiling the grandkids, then sending them home to their parents."

"I like that," Robert agreed.

"Those dreams sound like an excellent place to start," the Architect said. "What else do you see?"

"Well," Robert said, furrowing his brow. "I'd like to see the world, cross off a few countries on the old bucket list."

"That sounds nice," Jenny agreed. "Put me down for that one too."

"It does sound nice, doesn't it?" the Architect said. "Now, you've told me about the highlights of your retirement—the retirement dream. However, you won't spend your entire retirement golfing, visiting grandkids, or tanning on foreign beaches. So, now I want to know about the day-to-day. What does that look like? What do you do when it's too rainy to golf? Or on the weekend your grandchildren are out of town, and you can't visit them? What happens on those days?"

"I'd probably catch up on thirty years of too little sleep," Robert said, laughing.

"All right," the Architect said, laughing along with him. "I like the sound of that. What else?"

"Well, when we're both retired," Jenny said, "our schedules will line up more often, so we'll be able to go out together more. I'd love to have more date nights."

Robert squeezed her hand. "I second that."

"Spend more time together," the Architect summarized, "perfect."

"Other than that, we just want to live life to the fullest," Jenny said. "Maybe a few hikes throughout the week, evening walks around the neighborhood, scenic Sunday drives. We like to travel and golf, but we also enjoy the simple joys in life."

"Great," the Architect said. "Now, go ahead and open your eyes."

The Architect was holding a page in a notebook out for them to see. On the paper was a hastily sketched blueprint of an unfinished house. It featured a strong structural design unlike the beginning pictures on the walls.

"What is this?" Jenny asked curiously.

"Based on your description," the Architect said, "this is your Financial House."

"This doesn't look finished, though," Robert said, pointing to the light sketch on the blueprint.

"Well, of course not," the Architect said. "I can't complete an entire Financial House design based only on some dreams and ideas, can I? We must create a detailed plan to make those retirement dreams materialize."

"Okay, how do we do that?" Jenny asked.

"We build your Financial House the same way we'd build a real house," the Architect said. "We start at the bottom and build our way up. Let's get started, shall we?"

"We're ready," Jenny said enthusiastically. Robert nodded in agreement.

Questions to Consider

1. What are your big retirement dreams? Do you want to travel? Pursue new or old hobbies? Spend time with family?

____

____

____

____

2. What about your day-to-day activities? What does an average day in your retirement look like?

____

____

____

____

3. Are you ready to take the necessary steps to create the retirement lifestyle you've outlined above?

____

____

____

____

____

THE BLUEPRINT — CASH FLOW

"We've talked a little bit about your dreams and what you want your day-to-day life to look like in retirement," the Architect said. "But, before we begin outlining the fine details of your Financial House, I'd like to share one of the most important perspectives you must understand as you begin."

"And what is that?" Jenny asked.

"Well, you wouldn't design a house without choosing a plot of land to build on, would you?" the Architect inquired.

"No," Jenny replied. "Location is the first rule of real estate after all."

"Well, choosing a plot for your Financial House means having a firm understanding of your cash flow and what cash flow circumstances can affect your retirement income. Once you're equipped with that knowledge, designing the rest of your Financial House becomes much easier."

"Okay," Robert said. "I'm excited to learn."

"What factors do you think could greatly affect your cash flow?" the Architect asked.

"The first thing that comes to mind is inflation," Robert said. "Even if we have the cash flow to retire now, what happens in five to ten years when gas prices or grocery costs double due to steadily rising costs?"

"I worry about that too," Jenny added, "but I'm also concerned our Social Security checks won't be enough to cover the difference between our savings and what we might need going forward. Robert has a pension, but I'm not certain even that will be enough to bridge the gap."

"Those are valid concerns," the Architect agreed solemnly. "Understanding your cash flow and how it can fluctuate better prepares you for incidents that could unexpectedly interrupt your lifestyle. That's why, even though every Financial House is different, I always go through the process the same way— from the ground up." He made a few quick sketch marks on their blueprint, highlighting the different areas they would be designing.

"To start, we're going to build four cornerstones that will help to protect you and your assets," he continued.

"With our cornerstones in place, we build the Foundation which offers you emotional protection by creating an income plan you can't outlive.

Next, we raise the Walls that provide principal protection on your savings and investments.

Building the Beams of your Financial House ensures that you're not paying more than your fair share in taxes.

Finally, the Roof offers you the potential for growth through additional investments.

He moved the sketch over to Robert and Jenny for inspection. They noted that each section of the blueprint now showed arrows and labels for the crucial parts of the Financial House.

"Understanding cash flow is absolutely key," the Architect added. "Your Financial House needs careful construction that factors in cash flow concerns such as inflation, Social Security, pensions, and more. A lack of cash flow management could cause issues in every crucial area of your Financial House, throwing a wrench in your retirement plan."

"Okay," Robert said, pondering. "That makes sense."

"The second factor that can significantly affect your retirement is taxes," the Architect added. "Taxes right now are at record lows. In fact, they haven't been this low since the Great Depression. Well, besides a three-year period in the late '80s. During that time, lawmakers created a flat tax rate of 25 percent and claimed the U.S. would never again have to raise taxes."

"Never again only lasted three years?" Jenny asked skeptically, shaking her head in disbelief.

"That's right," the Architect said. "Our country's economy is always moving, so another 'never again' scenario is quite unlikely to occur. Let's talk about taxes, though. In your opinion, considering the current state of the world, do you think taxes are going up or down in the future?"

"My guess is up," Jenny replied.

"That's my belief as well," the Architect said. "To be clear, I can't predict the future. No one can. Let's imagine that taxes do go up. If you're currently in a 15 percent tax bracket and your income tax increases to 25 percent, you may find yourself needing to withdraw an extra 10 to 20 percent to make up that difference in income. How soon could that extra percentage withdrawn deplete your retirement account?

"That small increase doesn't seem like much when we're just using percentages, does it? So, instead, let's put it in real terms. Robert, you mentioned that you wanted to spend more time golfing in retirement. What if you could only afford to go half as often as you planned to? Jenny, you mentioned spending more time with family. What if that increase meant you'd need to cut out one or two family visits per year?"

"That's a sobering thought," Robert said. "We'd have to sacrifice the things that we enjoy, the reasons we want to retire in the first place. I mean, that's why we've been so hesitant to just retire."

Jenny nodded.

The Architect waved a hand over the blueprint. "That's why I don't like to discuss specific products, fees, or investing until you fully understand your cash flow and the percentage of your income that goes toward taxes. You need to be comfortable with that before moving forward."

"You're bringing up a lot of the reasons we've been so nervous about starting that next chapter in our lives," Robert said, a bit frustrated. "So, what can we do to get comfortable?"

"I understand. These concerns are real, and with all the sources of information available, making a decision can be difficult. Let me share my design process with you," the Architect said reassuringly. "Let's start with the Cornerstones."

Summary

- Taxes and inflation could play an important role in the success or failure of your retirement plan.
- Healthcare, your investments, and the state of the market also play a critical role in your overall plan.

Questions to Consider

1. How would inflation affect your cash flow/retirement income?

____

____

____

____

____

2. Do you believe tax rates will increase in the future? If so, are you prepared for the increase to affect your retirement income?

____

____

____

3. Do you know how much income and cash flow you will need to maintain the lifestyle you want?

____

____

Notes

THE CORNERSTONES

Chapter Four

THE FIRST CORNERSTONE — CASH RESERVES & DEBT

The Architect snapped his fingers. The living room dissolved around them, the walls and ceiling suddenly gone, revealing a sunny sky. Blinking in the bright light, Jenny and Robert examined their new surroundings. They stood on what looked like a preliminary construction site. Lumber and rocks sat on the sides of a wide, cleared plot of land, depressed about two feet below ground level.

Robert and Jenny looked around in surprise. Robert leaned down and touched the ground, making sure it was real.

"But…?" Jenny asked, taking in every detail. "How did you do that?"

"What better place to design a financial house than on your own residential plot?" the Architect asked with a secretive grin. "This is where we'll be constructing your personal financial house." As he spoke, he motioned to a drafting table with blank blueprints on its surface.

"I guess you're right," Robert said, still confused.

"Come, join me," the Architect said, gesturing for them to stand beside the drafting table. As they approached, they watched the Architect carefully sketch a large rectangular outline along one of the blueprint sheets.

"We start with the cornerstones," the Architect said. "Every cornerstone plays a critical role in supporting your Financial House. The first cornerstone we're going to discuss today is the **Cash Reserves and Debt Cornerstone.** This first cornerstone serves to protect you from the financial impact of unexpected costs that may arise throughout your lifetime."

"You mean emergencies?" Robert added.

"Well, yes, emergencies can play a major role here," the Architect said, "although, to me, the word *emergency* carries negative connotations as if it only references something dangerous or perhaps even life-threatening. Not all unexpected expenses can be defined that way. Sometimes an unexpected cost can be something as simple as your water heater going out, or your car needing extra maintenance. These aren't necessarily emergencies, but they can be urgent. Your Cash Reserves ensure that you can take care of these things sooner rather than later. Having a cash reserve can help lighten your financial burden and stress."

"No kidding," Robert said. "We've had our share of unexpected issues come up."

"Of course you have," the Architect said, "haven't we all? As the late great John Lennon once said, 'Life is what happens when you're busy making other plans.' That's why it's important to establish an extra financial cushion to fall back on when those unexpected bumps in the road happen. And, that's why having that first Cornerstone of Cash Reserves is so important."

"We have some money put away in a savings account," Jenny said, "but we're not sure if we have enough. How much *cushion* do you recommend?"

"That really depends on you," the Architect said. "After all, everyone's lifestyle and needs look different. That said, I generally recommend that you have at least three months' income set aside in an easily accessible account, like a savings account. It's even better if you can aim to save three to twelve months' income. That way, no matter what life throws at you, you're financially prepared to cover your basic needs and essentials while you get back on track."

"That adds up," Jenny said, nodding. "We're pretty close to having a year's income set aside. Let me ask you this, though: Wouldn't it be even better to continue saving even after we meet that benchmark?"

"Ah. While it's important to keep your coffers full, you don't necessarily want them overflowing," the Architect replied. "In the case of cash reserves, you *can* have too much of a good thing. That's the other side of the coin. If you keep too much in your cash reserves, you run the risk of missing out on potential growth and gains that you could have received from investing. After all, what interest rate is your bank offering on a standard savings account these days?"

"Point taken," Robert said. "They're not offering much."

"No, they're not," the Architect said. "Your money can be put to better use elsewhere."

"In that case, couldn't we benefit from putting all our savings into those higher earning accounts?" Jenny asked curiously.

"Remember," the Architect replied, "the primary purpose of your cash reserves isn't to grow your assets. Those dollars are purely there to be easily accessible in case of an unexpected expense or emergency. That way you don't have to pay early withdrawal fees or sacrifice your interest because you need to take the money out of a potentially higher earning investment account that hasn't reached its maturity date yet."

"That makes sense," Jenny replied.

"Wonderful," the Architect said. "Now, this cornerstone isn't *only* about your cash reserves, though that is a big part of it. It's also about your outstanding debts."

"Oh boy," Robert said, "I must be honest. Debt isn't my favorite topic of conversation."

"I think most people would agree with you," the Architect said. "As unpleasant as the topic may be, it's still important to assess where you stand on the path toward debt elimination. Debt will have a direct effect on your cash flow. After all, every dollar allocated toward paying off your debts is one dollar you don't have in your cash flow. That's why it's important to make a plan for eliminating your debt."

"You mean like a budget?" Jenny asked. "Though we don't like to have one, that's all under control."

"Glad to hear it," the Architect said. "Balancing your income and expenses is a critical piece of a successful income plan. Especially once you retire. After that, you don't have as much room for those 'oops' moments."

"I guess that's true," Robert said.

"We'll dive deeper into your income plan as we start building your Foundation, but for now, let's talk about those outstanding debts," the Architect said. "Living debt-free gives you absolute financial freedom. That would be the ideal way to retire: free to use your money as you wish. Still, life doesn't always go according to plan."

"You can say that again," Robert said, ruefully.

"Though debt-free living is always the ideal situation," the Architect elaborated, "debt isn't always bad. Debt can be used to create otherwise unavailable opportunities. Owning a home provides equity, and the loan you take could potentially be tax-deductible. Taking on debt to open a business and follow your dream could allow you to pursue your passion as a career."

"True," Jenny agreed. "I'd never thought of debt that way."

"The issues with debt arise when we spend money we don't have on things we don't really need," the Architect said. "Going into debt for a newer, shinier car is different than buying an affordable car that you need right now. Remember, if you have your cash reserves established, you should be able to pick up a reasonably priced car that gets you from point A to point B while you save up for that dream car if you wish.

"Another example is home maintenance. Of course, home repairs may pop up from time to time, and debt may be necessary. I'm not saying you should wait until you have the money to repair a pipe that's actively flooding your basement. However, you may want to hold off on putting in brand new cabinets until you've paid off your mortgage."

"New cabinets?" Robert asked, laughing. "When Jenny says new cabinets, she means a whole kitchen remodel. It's never just one project with any home renovation, is it?"

"No, it's not," the Architect said, shaking his head with a grin. "That's why it's so important to consider every factor before taking on new debt."

"You're right," Jenny said. "I do want that new kitchen, but I suppose we don't need the extra financial strain." She winked at her husband.

The Architect laughed. "I think we're ready." He sketched a cornerstone in the lower left corner of the blueprint outline he'd drawn earlier. Magically, the earth beneath them began to rumble. Jenny cried out and Robert gripped the drafting table. The Architect pointed to their left as a thick rectangular stone appeared solidly in the corner of the construction site. Jenny looked at the blueprint and back at the new cornerstone in surprise.

"Well, it looks like we've got quite a lot to do," Jenny said a little breathlessly, "but we're ready to keep going."

"Great," the Architect said. "Lao Tzu once said, '*The journey of a thousand miles begins with a single step.*' And this financial house has begun with your First Cornerstone. With proper planning and a little guidance, we can make your financial plan a reality."

Summary

- It's important to have three to twelve months of income in cash reserves, saved in an easily accessible account.
- Don't over-save. Once you have a comfortable amount in your cash reserves set aside (no more than twelve months' income), the rest of your savings should be put to work toward investment growth.
- Being debt-free is ideal, but you can build debt repayment into your retirement income plan if needed (so long as you have the income available to cover said debts).

Questions to Consider

1. Do you have at least three months of income in an easily accessible account in case of unexpected expenses?

____

____

2. Are you missing out on growth opportunities by over-saving instead of investing?

____

____

3. Are you on par to eliminate the entirety of your debt before you retire?

____

____

4. Are you going into debt for unnecessary purchases?

____

____

Notes

Chapter Five

THE SECOND CORNERSTONE – TO YOUR HEALTH

The Architect walked over to the newly manifested cornerstone and patted it with his hand, as if to prove it was there. He tilted his head back, admiring their work thus far. "The next cornerstone I want to discuss with you is the **Health Care, Long-Term Care, and Life Insurance Cornerstone**," he said.

"Healthcare is one topic we know plenty about," Jenny said. "As soon as we retire, we're trading in Robert's employer-provided healthcare for Medicare."

"That's one piece of an overall plan," the Architect replied. "Still, there's more to health care than just switching from traditional coverage to Medicare. Traditional Medicare, or Parts A and B, will generally cover eighty percent of your costs. That still leaves twenty percent that will come out of your pocket. Since healthcare costs are rising, that means you may need to do some additional planning. For example, were you aware that Fidelity's annual Retiree Health Care Cost Estimate states that a 65-year-old couple who retired in 2021 should expect to spend around $300,000 on healthcare over their lifetime?[1] Even funding twenty percent of that can weigh heavily on your retirement income."

"Wow," Robert said, shaking his head in disbelief. "I mean, we hear all the time that healthcare costs are rising, but hearing the actual numbers…" His voice trailed off as he let out an exaggerated breath, "It's simply overwhelming!"

"It can be," the Architect agreed solemnly. "Luckily, there are several Medicare coverage options to consider. Do you know what coverage you'll need in the future?"

"I think we're both in relatively good health," Robert said, "so I don't think we need to do much research."

"Actually," Jenny said, grabbing her husband's hand, "if you don't mind, Rob, I'd really like to know more. This has been something I've been worried about for quite a while now. Do you remember when my parents' health began to fail? They both had serious health concerns and eventually needed round-the-clock care. Those first weeks of constant care were a nightmare for me and my siblings. With careers and families of our own, we couldn't give Mom and Dad the level of care they needed, and we ultimately decided they needed an assisted living facility for their last few years."

---

[1] https://www.fidelity.com/viewpoints/personal-finance/plan-for-rising-health-care-costs

"I'm sorry to hear that, Jenny," the Architect said. "You're right, after all. You two may be healthy right now, but as Jenny just mentioned, the older you get, the more your health can suffer. Even those with ideal health may see deterioration over time physically and mentally, so it's important to weigh your options carefully before making any decisions with Medicare. Of course, your coverage can be adjusted each year as new needs arise, so long as you're healthy, but it's important to plan for the future."

Robert nodded.

"Jenny, you mentioned your parents," the Architect said, furrowing his brow and turning to her. "I know it may not be what you want to hear, but it's important to consider your family's medical history when making these decisions. While lifestyle choices can affect our health for better or worse, certain conditions and illnesses can run in the family as well. Doing a little homework never hurts. You can ask your doctor to check for cancer, arthritis, dementia, diabetes, or autoimmune disorders, among other common health issues that may be hereditary."

"You're right," Jenny said. "Is there anything else we should know about healthcare?"

"Absolutely," the Architect replied. "The Medicare program has additional coverage options to consider as well. For example, if you can attribute your good health to your medications, it may be worth your time to pay an additional cost for the Medicare Prescription Drug Plan, also known as Part D. This program can assist you in covering the costs of your prescriptions. You may want to seriously consider enrolling in Part D early because you'll be penalized every month you're eligible with higher premiums should you choose to enroll later."

"I guess we didn't know as much about Medicare as we thought," Jenny said.

"In that case, allow me to explain some alternative Medicare coverage options to you now," the Architect said. "First, there are Medicare Supplements. These are federally regulated Medicare plans purchased through private insurance companies, but the coverage is the same no matter which carrier you choose. Medicare Supplement plans have no networks, and they cover all medical costs to close that twenty percent gap we discussed earlier. Some supplemental programs may offer foreign travel emergency benefits as well. That tends to look good to couples wanting to get out and see the world in their retirement years.

"Another option would be Medicare Advantage Plans which are run by private insurance companies but function more like traditional health insurance policies. They have deductibles, in and out of network costs, and out-of-pocket maximums. Deductibles, coverage, and services offered to you may vary between plans. These plans will sometimes offer additional benefits such as vision, hearing, or dental that you wouldn't usually get through traditional Medicare or a supplemental plan. These policies generally cost less than Medicare Supplement plans, but choosing a Medicare Advantage plan initially means you'd have to go through medical underwriting for approval if you choose to switch to a Medicare Supplement program later. You could be declined based on your health conditions at the time. That's why it's important to plan ahead and understand which plans appeal to you.

"Interesting," Jenny said, crossing her arms. "I hadn't realized Medicare was such an extensive program. I guess we need to put a little more thought into our Medicare options before we make that switch."

"It can be daunting, yes," the Architect said, "but equipped with an intimate knowledge of your healthcare needs and with the right guidance, you can choose the right plan. You can sometimes adjust the Medicare Advantage plan and Part D coverage as needed during the open enrollment windows available to you annually. Still, it's important to consider which choices may become unavailable to you as time goes on."

As he finished speaking, another rumble shook the ground. Jenny reflexively grabbed Rob's arm as a second cornerstone appeared in the corner adjacent to the first. This cornerstone was smaller with crumbling edges on two sides as if it were only a fraction of the size it should have been.

"What's wrong with the cornerstone?" Rob asked.

"Well, did you assume we were finished building it? Sorry to disappoint, but Medicare and healthcare insurance aren't all the second cornerstone is about. We have much more to discuss."

"What else is there?" Jenny asked, curious.

"Well, Jenny," the Architect replied, "I'm sure you can answer that. You mentioned that your parent's health deteriorated quickly. So, what happens if your health deteriorates similarly, so much so that you can no longer take care of yourself?"

Jenny's eyes brimmed with tears. "I'll be honest, this is a big concern for me. It broke my heart to watch my parents struggle to accept that they just couldn't do things on their own anymore. Especially my poor father; he was such a proud man. I guess I'm scared that something similar could happen to me. I don't want to go through all that because I know what an emotional and financial burden that would be on Robert."

"The same could happen to me," Robert said, holding his wife's hand. "Sweetheart, you know I'll always take care of you as long as I'm able." Turning to the Architect, he added, "I agree, the financial burden does concern me too. My in-laws' savings were drained month after month until there was nothing left. Fortunately, we were able to help a little. Jenny's siblings pitched in what they could, but that does concern me going forward. If something were to happen, and Jenny and I needed care, I wouldn't want to settle for a lower quality of care or have our children shoulder that burden for us."

"It sounds like you both loved your parents and wanted the best possible care," the Architect surmised. "That said, it couldn't have been cheap. And it certainly couldn't have been easy to watch your parents suffer like that."

Jenny wiped a tear away from her eye. "What can we do?"

The Architect handed her a handkerchief from his pocket. "To make sure this never happens to you or Robert, let's discuss Long-Term-Care Insurance. Now, not everyone will need this type of coverage, but it's something you need to seriously consider, nonetheless. While your parents' story is tragic, they weren't alone. In fact, a recent study by Morningstar[2] stated that fifty-two percent of Americans turning age sixty-five will need Long-Term-Care at some point in their life. That's a little over half, so it's critical that you at least think about it as a part of your Health Care Cornerstone."

"I think you know how seriously I'll consider my options," Jenny said, smiling softly as she regained her composure.

The Architect smiled sympathetically. "It's a difficult conversation, but an important one. Let's talk about some of the costs that could come up within Long-Term-Care. Bear in mind, the numbers I'm going to share with you are based on national averages. These prices could vary based upon where you live. A private room in a nursing home could potentially cost you over $7,500 a month[3]. For a semi-private room, you might pay just shy of $7,000 per month. Even for an assisted living facility like the one you mentioned your parents were in, you're looking at over $3,500 per month. And that's just the price for the rooms. There are other costs as well—health

---

[2] Must-Know Statistics About Long-Term Care: 2019 Edition | Morningstar
[3] Must-Know Statistics About Long-Term Care: 2019 Edition | Morningstar

aides, homemakers, adult day health care. Those costs can add up, especially over time. After all, it's called Long-Term Care for a reason. Without the proper coverage, those costs can really make a dent in your Financial House, shaking the very foundation of the financial plan you've worked so hard to build."

"So, what do Long-Term Care policies cost?" Jenny asked.

"That's a great question, Jenny," the Architect said, "and one that's not simple to answer. Many variables play into the price, such as the age at which you apply for the policy, and your health records to name a few. The average premium for a 55-year-old couple is around $3,050 per year[4]. Keep in mind, that's less than most life insurance and healthcare premiums for a couple that age. More importantly, it's less than the cost of a single month's stay at many assisted living facilities."

"That's definitely something we'll look into," Robert said.

"Should you ever need long-term-care," the Architect added, "you'll be tested on the six ADLs, or Activities of Daily Living, so your care can be accurately assessed."

"What are these activities?" Jenny asked.

"The Activities of Daily Living are the daily tasks you need to be able to perform independently to live on your own. The six ADLs are eating, bathing, dressing, toileting, transferring, and continence. In other words, you need to be able to feed yourself, bathe yourself, dress yourself, use the restroom, move from a standing position to a sitting position to a lying position and vice versa, and control your bladder and bowels. You need to be able to do these things without assistance from others."

"No thank you to any of that," Robert said. "I hope I stay healthy until the day I die."

---

[4] Health Insurance (thebalance.com)

"We should all be so lucky," the Architect said, "and hopefully you will be. We take these tasks for granted day in and day out when we're in great health. Still, knowing which of these activities require assistance from others will determine what type of care you'll require. And remember, we don't purchase insurance for the best-case scenario, do we?"

"Good point," Jenny said, laughing. "Still, it seems like a lot to invest if we never need to use it."

"I agree," the Architect said. "That's why it's great that there are many different options. There are a total of seven ways to fund your long-term-care policy. Another option is investing in a life insurance policy that offers long-term-care benefits. In many cases, life insurance will offer the option to use some or all of the life insurance benefits to help cover your long-term-care costs. This policy can be a good investment just in case you need long-term care coverage. If not, your heirs will still receive the death benefit from the life insurance policy."

"Oh, well that sounds a little more my speed," Jenny added excitedly.

"Well, don't fall in love with a plan just yet. Remember, we've had a brief discussion where I've shared just two options with you. There are several, and we'll review them before we complete this cornerstone." With another rumble, the second cornerstone grew dramatically, but it was still missing a large triangular chunk.

"I see we really do have a bit more to discuss," Robert said, frowning at the incomplete cornerstone.

"Which brings me to the third and final segment of our second cornerstone—Life Insurance," the Architect said. "As you mentioned, there are some incredible benefits that many people aren't aware of, so let's talk about a few of them."

"Besides an option for Long-Term-Care coverage," Robert said, "do people even use life insurance after retirement? I mean, our kids are all grown, and we've done our financial planning. Is life insurance even necessary at this stage of life?"

"That is certainly the most common reason to have life insurance—income replacement for survivors," the Architect said. "Many people think the way you do." He waved his hand for dramatic emphasis. "Sure, it's a great option for someone who's still in the workforce and needs to provide money for their family if they die, but not for us. However, there's more to income replacement than just replacing your paycheck.

"You see, when one of you dies, your financial situation can drastically change. For example, you'll lose the lesser of your two Social Security checks. If the spouse who dies had a pension, you may lose a portion or all of it, depending on how you have set up your pension benefits. Then, there's the question of taxes. As you return to single taxpayer filing status, your income could wind up in a higher tax bracket, meaning the percentage of tax you pay each year could increase. Life insurance helps offset that income and asset reduction. Even so, life insurance provides even more benefits."

"Like what?" Jenny asked.

"Well, what about settling your debts?" the Architect asked. "We talked about the importance of retiring debt-free, but how would you manage if you weren't debt-free and your spouse died? If you have credit card debt or a few payments left on your mortgage, a life insurance policy that pays those things off could give the surviving spouse a fresh start. It's already so emotionally difficult to lose a loved one. Life insurance can be helpful in giving the survivor time to grieve and process the loss without the added stress of excessive financial obligations."

"That makes sense," Robert said, looking at his wife. "What else can you use a life insurance policy for?"

"How about as an alternative tax-free investment?" the Architect suggested. "As you just pointed out, often when we hear the term 'life insurance' we think about the old life insurance policies that served only as income replacement upon our deaths. Like many financial programs and institutions, life insurance needed to evolve and adapt to what people needed. Modern-day life insurance has made some incredible adjustments to their program that add much-needed benefits."

"Adjustments?" Jenny asked. "Like what?"

"Well," the Architect replied, "your life insurance policy can now function similarly to a Roth IRA, with additional benefits. With a Roth IRA, you've already paid taxes on the money being invested, and therefore, your investment grows tax-free. Like a Roth IRA, you've already paid the tax on the premium you're paying into a life insurance policy. The cash value attached to that policy grows tax-free as long as you don't surrender the policy's contract!"

"I didn't know that," Robert said. "That sounds great!"

"What else?" Jenny asked excitedly.

"There are several other benefits to consider," the Architect said, "but I'm going to share just one more with you because it conveniently transitions to our third cornerstone. That benefit is the ability to use your life insurance policy to cover your funeral expenses. We'll jump to that in just a moment. First, let's make sure we've properly constructed this cornerstone."

As he finished speaking, the now familiar rumble of the ground set in. A moment later, the full, perfectly rectangular cornerstone appeared before them. Jenny sighed with satisfaction and turned back to the Architect, eager to learn more.

Summary

- At age sixty-five, you'll transition your healthcare coverage from traditional insurance coverage to Medicare.
- Since there are many Medicare programs, it's important to understand the costs and benefits of each one to choose the best plan for you.
- Medicare Supplemental and Medicare Advantage plans are options you can add to Medicare's traditional coverage, Parts A and B. Such plans may be beneficial to you depending on your health, the level of coverage you want, and the area in which you live.
- More than half of U.S. retirees turning sixty-five will need Long-Term-Care at some point.
- Long-Term Care insurance is one way to offset the costs of nursing homes, assisted living, home aides, etc.
- Life insurance can be used as an alternate method to fund your long-term-care insurance, provide tax-free income, bolster your income replacement, and cover debts upon your death.

Questions to Consider

1. Do you know your family's medical history? If so, have you taken that information into account as you plan for your healthcare coverage in retirement?

____

____

____

2. Do you have a plan to fund additional medical costs that traditional Medicare doesn't cover?

____

____

____

3. Have you considered a Medicare Supplement plan or a Medicare Advantage plan? Do you know the differences between the two?

____

____

____

4. Have you factored the possibility of Long-Term Care into your retirement plan?

5. Are you aware of all the options that can provide for the cost of Long-Term Care?

6. If you choose not to carry Long-Term Care Insurance, do you have an alternative financial plan to cover Long-Term Care?

7. Are you aware of the many benefits life insurance can offer in addition to income replacement?

Notes

Chapter Six

THE THIRD CORNERSTONE — PRE-PLANNING AND YOUR LEGACY

"Perhaps we should take a seat for this next discussion," the Architect began, motioning them over to a few stacked stools near the drafting table. Robert and Jenny took their seats and settled in. "Now that we've discussed the difficult topics of health care, long-term care, and life insurance, do you feel better knowing what you need to do to take care of yourselves and each other financially should something happen?"

"It's certainly not an easy topic," Jenny said. "But I do feel comfortable knowing that at least our finances can remain in order."

"That's a great feeling to have," the Architect sighed a bit and folded his hands together in his lap. "I hope you'll forgive me for our next discussion then," the Architect said, "because we're about to travel into even more difficult territory. Now, we're going to explore options that can lessen the financial burden as well as the difficulty of planning for your spouse and heirs when you pass away, or if your health fails entirely."

"I hope we're ready for this talk," Robert said, a little unsure. "Of course, no one lives forever, but I guess nobody likes to discuss their own death, or the death of loved ones." He reached out and squeezed his wife's hand, as much for his own sake as for hers.

"It's not a pleasant thought," Jenny agreed.

"You're right," the Architect said. "But still, it's an important conversation to have, especially while you're capable of sound decision-making."

"You're right," Jenny said. "It's better to figure out what we're doing now, rather than trying to figure it all out after something's happened."

"That's right," the Architect said. "Allow me to introduce our third step in building your Financial House: The Pre-Planning and Legacy Preparation Cornerstone. First, let's start where we left off in our second cornerstone discussion: life insurance. Remember, life insurance can be used to cover your final expenses. I want you to imagine that you've just lost your spouse. You have no idea what paperwork is needed or where said paperwork would even be, who to call and in what order, and you're not sure where, or even if, your spouse wanted to be buried. These would be difficult issues to combat especially at such a heartbreaking time.

"Perhaps instead of a burial, you would prefer cremation or a memorial service for your spouse. If you choose a traditional burial, you may find yourself overwhelmed by funeral home service quotes, casket prices, and the cost of a cemetery plot, let alone a headstone with a personalized engraving. Of course, all this stress adds to the most difficult part—you've just lost your life partner, and you need time to grieve."

"I'm already not liking this scenario," Jenny said, her voice breaking as she spoke, "for either of us. I don't want either of us to go through that."

"It sounds traumatic, doesn't it?" the Architect agreed. "Let's scratch that scenario. This time, imagine that you don't have to worry about the final expenses because your life insurance policy will cover most or all of the financial burden. You know exactly what your budget is should any balance remain. Additionally, imagine that you and your partner talked and prepared for this eventuality. In your filing cabinet or home safe you'll find a folder or binder with instructions, all necessary paperwork, names, and contact information for important parties. The stress just rolls off your shoulders, doesn't it? Instead, you have the time and energy to mourn and to celebrate the life you shared with your loved one."

"That sounds much better," Jenny said. "I mean, it's never going to be easy losing someone, especially my Rob." She looked at her husband and smiled. "But worrying about money or planning on top of that just sounds unbearable. I don't know if I'd be able to handle it all at once. Being prepared would give us some much-needed peace in such an emotionally difficult time."

"I agree," the Architect said, "which is why it's so important to do the proper planning now. I'd like to take this opportunity to talk to you about pre-planning as well. In addition to planning for your final expenses, let's talk about other ways you can plan ahead to reduce your loved ones' stress upon your passing."

"What exactly is pre-planning?" Robert asked. "Is that like our will and whatnot? I'd say we've done a good job for our family. Our will is in order, and we have burial plots paid for and reserved."

"Wow, many people don't even have that," the Architect said. "So, you're right, you have done a good job. Your will and burial plot are certainly important factors. But pre-planning deals much more with the personal side than the financial side. Benjamin Franklin once said, 'Nothing is certain, except death and taxes.' While many people properly plan for taxes, not many adequately plan for their death."

"That's true," Jenny agreed.

"Pre-planning, in my opinion, is one of the greatest gifts you can leave behind for your loved ones. You carefully prepare for your passing so your family can experience the second scenario we discussed. That way, when you die, your family isn't left scrambling or arguing over what they believe your wishes were. Instead, everything falls into place. Everyone knows what you wanted; they know who's in charge of executing your wishes; and they can focus on remembering what you meant to them."

"That sounds fantastic! What specific items should we focus on?" Jenny asked.

"Pre-planning entails gathering up your important documents—wills, trusts, and similar papers - then, putting them in one place or outlining their locations so the executor of your estate can easily find them. You gather your familial and financial information together with paperwork, phone numbers, account information, etc. You're basically compiling anything your spouse or heirs will need in the event of your death."

"Oh," Robert said, looking at his wife in dismay. "That's something we really need to do. I guess those details would be rather important."

"Pre-planning doesn't end there, though. You can also include a plan for your funeral services. If you know which funeral home you'd like to use, and where you'd like to be buried, you can make those arrangements now, before you pass. You can even pay in advance, so your heirs don't have to shoulder the cost while waiting for your life insurance to reimburse them."

"Wow," Jenny said. "Who knew there was so much planning to do? It's a lot to take in."

"It can be," the Architect said. "That's why it's so important to make these decisions while you're still here. Otherwise that burden falls on your spouse or children when you're gone. No one wants to think about dying or losing a spouse but making these decisions while you're healthy and cognizant is a critical piece of a complete financial plan."

"You're right," Robert said, putting a hand to his forehead. "I don't want you or the kids to struggle with that if I die first."

"I don't want that either," Jenny added.

"I'm so glad you two are on the same page," the Architect said. "That's crucial for this planning process. In addition to having your documents prepared, it's important for the two of you to discuss your wishes with each other. After all, odds are the two of you won't pass away together. One of you will most likely survive the other and be responsible, at least in part, for the funeral planning, estate distribution, etc. That's why it's important to stay on the same page by having these discussions, no matter how unpleasant."

"You're right," Jenny said, deep in thought. "We'll soldier through the talks. How do we get started, though? I'm not even sure I know what I want for *my own* funeral."

"It's not something we often consider. Let's practice another mental exercise. This one won't be as fun as imagining your dream retirement, but it's an exercise I believe is essential to pre-planning."

"We're ready," Robert said, closing his eyes. Jenny did the same.

"Okay," the Architect said, pausing for effect. "I want you to imagine the events after your death as if your wishes were being carried out exactly as you wanted. Are you being cremated or buried? If you've chosen to be buried, will you be buried in the local cemetery or in a family plot in your hometown? If you're being cremated, where will your ashes be laid to rest? Will they sit on one of your children's mantelpieces, or will they be scattered on the wind atop your favorite hiking mountain?

"What will the headstone that marks your resting place look like? Is it made of marble, granite, or fieldstone? Do you have a favorite quote, poem, or scripture engraved beside your name? Do you have those images in your mind?"

"Yes," Jenny said, her eyes remaining closed.

"Good," the Architect continued. "Now, let's move on to your funeral services. "Will your service be simple or extravagant? Will the service be held at your local church, a funeral home, or your own home? Who is overseeing the event? Is there a religious leader you'd like to preside over the service? Maybe your eldest child? Or a close friend? Which of the guests will share their memories of you? Will the pulpit be open to anyone? Will your children speak about your life and accomplishments? Will your close friends share their thoughts and feelings? Who will deliver your eulogy? Do you have a favorite song and someone in mind to perform it?"

The Architect paused a moment, letting his questions sink in. He sat in silence for a few minutes, allowing the couple to ponder all the questions he had asked them. He finally spoke. "Now, open your eyes."

They did so and looked at one another, sharing a brief yet emotional smile.

"That was a lot to process," Jenny said, wiping her eyes. Robert stood and embraced her. Jenny returned the hug, "I'm fine, I'm fine. Stop making a fuss."

"It can be a lot to process," the Architect said, smiling knowingly at her. "Losing someone you love is already so emotional, and those emotions can be even more heightened and strained when proper pre-planning hasn't been done. It puts an undue burden on our surviving family to make plans and decisions quickly and under great stress, all the while worrying if they're doing right by you."

"You're right! Dealing with both my parents' deaths was certainly stressful," Jenny said. "First, my father went. We had to search through his den for hours, trying to locate all the paperwork he had tucked away in various corners and files. We did our best to fulfill his wishes, but it wasn't easy to figure out. I wouldn't want my children or Robert to struggle the way I did."

"Certainly," Robert said. "I hope our children will be able to focus on how much we loved them and not worry about the nitty, gritty details."

"One of the greatest benefits of pre-planning," the Architect continued, "is that many mortuaries offer pre-planning packages, and you may be able to find discounted prices on funeral services, a casket, and other necessities, sometimes for pennies on the dollar compared to what your heirs would pay upon your passing. All you have to do is plan ahead for that eventuality."

"Now that's a benefit I can appreciate," Robert said.

"Absolutely," the Architect agreed.

"You mentioned preparing our legacy as part of this cornerstone as well," Jenny said. "What do you mean by that? Is that where our will comes in?"

"Let's talk about that for a bit," the Architect said, shifting on the stool. "Have you discussed the contents of your will with your children? Do they know what to expect? That discussion can be monumentally important to stop bickering and hurt feelings before they happen. Furthermore, are those documents—your will, trust, powers of attorney documents for finances and healthcare, etc.—easily accessible when your family needs them?

"Most of that stuff is in a file cabinet back home," Robert said, nodding. "It's more or less in the same place. After our talk today, I'll definitely organize it into one folder or binder as you've recommended."

"Do your children know where it is?" the Architect asked. "Do they know which drawer? Which files?"

"I guess we haven't shared that with them quite yet," Robert admitted. "Sounds like I've got some spring cleaning *and* a few tough conversations ahead of me."

"That's my cue to move on to discussing 'Legacy Preparation'," the Architect said. "Many people call it 'legacy planning,' but planning means setting intentions; preparing means taking action."

"Planning and preparing aren't the same thing." Jenny said. Guess we better roll up our sleeves and get to work."

The Architect smiled warmly. "That's a great attitude to have. Let me share a story with you. I had a dear friend who was quite the adventurer. In his retirement years, he bought himself an RV and headed out on the open road. He was always traveling, never in one place for too long. As he got older, however, his health deteriorated, and he began to slow down. He couldn't take care of himself alone on the open road anymore."

"How sad," Jenny said.

"It was," the Architect confirmed with a hint of melancholy in his eyes. "If we had our way, we would live long, full lives and pass away before our health began to impede our ability to do the things we love. Unfortunately, that's not how life works.

"My friend didn't die shortly after having to stop traveling. Instead, his situation slowly declined over the better part of a decade. At first, he just needed a little help here and there, so he moved closer to his family and found a nice, assisted living community for active seniors. It allowed him to be semi-independent while still having the support he needed with difficult tasks. A while later, he moved to assisted living, and eventually moved into a long-term-care facility where he spent the remainder of his life, nearly another five years."

"I'm so sorry to hear that," Jenny said. "That must have been hard for him."

"Thank you so much for your compassion," the Architect said, smiling wanly. "You needn't worry about my friend, though. While he would have preferred the open road, he was loved and well cared for, in no small part due to the documents that helped protect him throughout the process."

"Documents?" Robert asked, curious. "What kind of documents?"

"The Powers of Attorney, for one," the Architect replied. "Because my friend took the time to make arrangements, he knew he'd be taken care of in his senior years. He had designated one of his children to make medical decisions in his best interest. She attended doctors' appointments with him, helped oversee his care, and generally watched out for his overall wellbeing. He designated one of his sons to manage his finances for him. He monitored his accounts and investments, paid his bills and his taxes, and generally oversaw his finances. Together, these two Powers of Attorney were able to work together to ensure all decisions were made in my friend's best interest and in alignment with his wishes."

"Wouldn't it be simpler to use the same person for both tasks?" Robert asked. "Seems like that would cut back on any confusion."

"You absolutely could," the Architect affirmed, "and sometimes that may be your best, or only, option. However, if possible, I strongly recommend using two separate people. First, doing one of these jobs adds a lot of stress to one person's life, let alone both. To add both to one person's shoulders can be overwhelming. Second, your children may have different skill sets and strengths. Perhaps, one of your children has the patience and compassion to deal with doctors day-in and day-out, while another child may have the fiscal know-how to expertly manage your money."

"Come to think of it, that makes perfect sense," Jenny said. "Our daughter is very kindhearted and loving, but she can be a little scatterbrained sometimes. Our son is a shrewd businessman, so he'd be better with the numbers."

"Sometimes it's an easy straightforward decision to make," the Architect said. "Other times the choice can be more difficult. Above all else, these Powers of Attorney should go to someone you trust, someone who will put your best interests first when making decisions regarding your health and finances. Having the skillset is important but being trustworthy of your care when you're no longer able to care for yourself is critical."

"That makes sense to me," Robert said. "What's next?"

"Next, let's discuss the importance of wills and trusts. Your will, as I'm sure you know, designates who will inherit ownership of your assets and possessions after you've passed on. But consider this: not everything your children want to inherit is based on monetary value. Perhaps your son asks about the grandfather clock you inherited from *your* father whenever he's visiting your home. Maybe your daughter loves to cook with you, and your collection of old cookbooks would mean the world to her. Whether based on sentimental or monetary value, your designations are quite important to avoid family feuds and keep your passing as smooth as possible."

"Of course," Jenny said. "We know how important wills are. We had ours drawn up quite a few years ago."

"Great," the Architect said. "Let's go more in-depth then. Did you know that the property you designate to your heirs in your will must go through probate first?"

"Probate?" Robert repeated, groaning.

"I see that word stirs up some bad feelings," the Architect said. "Are you imagining nightmarish legal battles and arguments? In reality, probate is just a fancy legal term for executing your will. A judge checks the validity of your will and grants permission for the assets to be distributed as you've outlined."

"I've heard it takes a lot of time to get sorted out, though," Jenny said. "There's no way to avoid probate?"

"Let me address your time concern first," the Architect said. "You're right, probate can potentially take some time. On average, assets remain in probate around two years after your passing.[5] There are several factors at play when considering the length of probate: the amount in assets you're passing down, any debts and taxes you may owe, how many heirs you've listed, and even whether any of your heirs wish to contest the will. Based on these and many other factors, the time you're really looking at can vary from six months to several years."

Robert groaned again, emphasizing his disapproval.

"I can see you're not a fan of the process, Robert," the Architect said, smiling. "You'll be glad to hear this next bit then. There is a way to potentially avoid probate altogether using a living trust. You see, when you place your assets in a trust, you no longer own them—the trustee of the trust does. Of course, both of you would be the trustees at first and would still maintain control of the assets until you die or are unable to manage them. At that point your Power of Attorney would manage the assets for you. Generally, when you die, your property goes through probate, so by placing your property into a trust, you can potentially avoid the probate process."

"Great!" Robert exclaimed enthusiastically. "Now you've piqued my interest."

"Of course," the Architect continued, "you may still require a simple will to cover any assets not included in your trust. However, if your significant properties are transferred

---

[5] https://estate.findlaw.com/probate/probate-process-and-timeline.html

into the trust, your other assets shouldn't be held up in probate."

"That sounds amazing. Do you have any tips about setting up inheritance? We want to ensure our kids get the money we leave behind for them." Jenny asked. "A friend of mine had parents who made some financial mistakes, and her inheritance wound up in someone else's hands. I don't want some error we've made to cost our children their inheritance."

"One big tip," the Architect replied. "About eight out of every ten people I visit with have set up their beneficiaries incorrectly. Sometimes it's been a small mistake and is therefore a simple fix. Other times we've found some bigger mistakes that needed immediate, detailed correction."

"Sounds like you've got some stories," Jenny said.

"Indeed, I do," the Architect said with a small laugh. "Can you imagine how you'd feel if your husband had just passed away, and you discovered that some of his assets had been left to someone else by mistake? Maybe he listed his parents before you were married and forgot to update them. Or worse still, what if an ex-spouse had not been properly removed as a beneficiary? Laws exist in about half of the states that revoke beneficiary designations upon a divorce statute, but some may still allow an ex-spouse to inherit assets."

Jenny slapped her husband's arm playfully. "I'd be livid!"

"I haven't done that," Robert said, shaking his head and rubbing his arm jokingly as if in real pain. "Why are you getting mad at me?"

The Architect chuckled. "You may be right, Robert, but you'd be surprised how often little mistakes happen that can cause truly painful family rifts. So, let's discuss what you can do with your retirement accounts and life insurance to make sure this doesn't happen to you."

"Sounds like I better pay attention," Robert said, winking at Jenny.

They all laughed.

"First thing - be sure you name a primary beneficiary," the Architect said.

"Well, of course," Jenny said, scoffing.

"It may seem obvious," the Architect replied, "but you'd be surprised how many people make this mistake. They assume their assets will go to their spouse or children by default. Generally, the financial company handling your accounts will have default guidelines. If you haven't designated a beneficiary, most companies will usually transfer the assets into your estate. That means those assets will most likely spend time in..." he exaggerated his pause, looking at Robert.

"Probate," Robert chimed in, following it up with the expected groan.

"I'm pretty sure we've handled that part correctly," Jenny said. "At least, I hope so. It wouldn't hurt to double check, though."

"That brings up another item to consider regarding your legacy," the Architect said. "Make sure you have the *right* beneficiary named. For example, if your son is a Junior or Third, you would want to designate that specifically on the document, so your financial executors don't mistakenly skip over him, believing the assets were to be left to you, Robert, upon your wife's passing."

Jenny's eyes widened. "We better check on that one."

"Updating your beneficiaries also means, as our story showed, changing names when major life events occur such as new marriages, divorces, births, and deaths. For example, if your daughter gets married, her last name will likely change, and you'll need to update that information. A divorce would change that back. Though some states automatically revoke beneficiary status upon divorce, it's important to work with a Financial Architect and estate attorney who are familiar with your state's laws. Consider this too as your family grows. What if you forget to name your youngest grandchildren in the will? If you've designated your assets to be left to your children, and one of them dies before you, their children may miss out if your beneficiaries aren't set up correctly. That's why it's important to assess any new events happening in your life and adjust your documents as needed."

"I'll double-check first thing when I get home," Robert said.

"Keeping up with your beneficiaries protects the feelings and relationships of the family you leave behind," the Architect continued. "It ensures no one is overlooked, left out, or inherits more or less than you intended."

"My goodness, missing someone in our will would break my heart," Jenny said. "We'll make sure that doesn't happen. Can you possibly take a closer look to double-check our work?"

"I'd be happy to help," the Architect said, "because there is so much room for error, a Financial Architect like myself who understands the process can review your forms with you and make sure your wishes are carried out exactly as you've intended."

"I'd better get on that," Robert said, smiling at his wife.

"Oh, just one more thing," the Architect added. "In certain cases, you can arrange for your assets to be passed down in increments."

"Increments?" Jenny asked, puzzled. "What do you mean? Why would we do that?"

"Well," the Architect replied, imagine all the money you worked hard for your entire life. You sacrificed so you could save, you studied the market, or worked with professionals like myself to make better investments. All that time and effort so you could enjoy your retirement and perhaps leave a little behind to your heirs. Then imagine after they receive it, every dollar could be gone in five years or less.

"What!" Jenny exclaimed. "No, that couldn't happen. Who would be that wasteful?"

"Actually, the Architect said reluctantly, "studies show that the average inheritance is gone within the first five years due to the inheritor's careless spending or bad investment decisions."[6]   To avoid that outcome, you can make arrangements that allow you to leave your money, or at least a portion of your assets, to your heirs in increments. They can receive a portion of their inheritance at age thirty-five, forty-five, fifty-five, and so on. That way, you can provide an inheritance for your children while still protecting your hard-earned estate."

"Our kids are usually pretty responsible," Jenny said, "Is that really something we need to worry about?"

Robert gave her a funny look. "Whose kids are you talking about?"

The Architect laughed. "You don't agree, Robert?"

"I love our kids," he replied defensively, "and Jenny's right. They can be responsible when they need to be. Still, I know they tend to spend a little more on their luxuries than we do, certainly more than they probably should. That's their right, of course. Still, it's their right because it's their money. This is our money, though, so I'm glad we have some different options."

"There's a general rule I'd consider as you set up an inheritance for your heirs," the Architect said. "It's a simple question you ask yourself: Would you help them with that today?"

"Today?" Jenny asked. "What do you mean by that?"

"Yes, today," the Architect replied. "Heaven forbid, if your son suffered an accident and needed money to help cover his medical expenses, I'm sure you'd probably pull some money out of your retirement accounts to help him recover. And, if you could afford it, you'd probably even give him a little cushion to help him get back on his feet."

---

[6] https://www.betterment.com/resources/received-an-inheritance/

"Without hesitation," Robert said. "If we had the money, we'd help. At the end of the day, our children are everything. They're our real legacy."

"Then let's use another example. Let's imagine he's not hurt but his car has broken down, and he needs a new vehicle for work. He comes to you and asks for help to purchase a new car."

"I'm sure if we had the extra money," Jenny said, "we'd be willing to help. We could probably loan him a few thousand. He needs to get to work after all."

"But what if he told you he didn't want just an extra $10,000 for a car in good condition, but instead he wanted a newer car, so he needed a $30,000 loan?" the Architect asked.

"I'd say 'nice try,'" Robert said, chuckling.

The Architect nodded. "That's exactly my point. My general rule of thumb is this: if you wouldn't help them with it now, while you're still alive, don't enable that kind of careless financial behavior after you're gone."

"You're right," Jenny said. "That makes perfect sense."

"Plus," the Architect said, "there's a great reason to set it up this way that also benefits your inheritors. In many cases, the inheritance you leave can continue to grow. By limiting the amount your heirs receive up front, they could potentially inherit even more over their lifetime."

"So, it's a win-win," Robert said, smiling.

"It looks like you two really understand the importance of our Pre-Planning and Legacy Cornerstone," the Architect said, his words seemingly summoning another miniature earthquake. As they sat there, a wide, solid cornerstone appeared in a third corner of their building plot.

"It looks like we're almost done with these cornerstones," Jenny said excitedly. "I can't wait for the next one."

Summary

- Life insurance can serve as income replacement for the surviving spouse, debt settlement, and/or coverage of pre-planning expenses.
- Pre-planning can help you reduce the planning and financial stress left to your loved ones after you've passed away.
- Discuss the contents of your will with your children and/or heirs, so everyone has proper expectations.
- Using Trust documents can help you avoid probate.
- Powers-of-Attorney offer financial, legal, and medical protection for you if you become incapable of handling your own affairs.
- Update or review your beneficiaries regularly as major life events occur such as marriages, divorces, new births, or deaths.
- You can leave your inheritance behind in increments, so your legacy isn't spent in five years or less.

Questions to Consider

1. Were you aware that you can potentially use life insurance to cover your funeral expenses?

____

2. Have you taken the time to do the proper pre-planning so your wishes can be carried out for your passing, your funeral, your service, etc.?

____

3. Do you have someone (preferably two individuals) to whom you can entrust your Powers of Attorney for medical and financial matters when the time comes?

____

____

4. Have you discussed your funeral, estate, and legacy wishes with your children, executor, and/or those chosen to act with Powers of Attorney?

____

5. Are your beneficiaries set up correctly?
   a. Do you have a primary beneficiary and a secondary beneficiary designated? Do you have any other additional beneficiaries?

____

____

____

   b. Have any births, deaths, marriages, divorces, or other events occurred that would change the way your beneficiaries should be arranged?

____

____

____

6. Were you aware that you can leave your assets to your heirs in increments over the course of their lifetime?

____

____

____

Notes

Chapter Seven

THE FOURTH CORNERSTONE – HOME, AUTO, AND UMBRELLA INSURANCE

The Architect walked back over to the blueprints, allowing the couple to take a better look at the page. "You've come a long way."

"We have," Jenny said, "but I'm excited to learn about this last cornerstone as well."

"Let's dive right in then, shall we? Our fourth and final cornerstone is the **Home, Auto, and Umbrella Insurance Cornerstone.**"

"This is one cornerstone we're quite familiar with," Robert said. "We've owned homes most of our lives, and driven cars for even longer."

"I'm glad to hear it," the Architect said, smiling at him. "Let's start with Homeowners' Insurance."

"We've got some," Jenny said. "Our bank requires that we carry Homeowners' Insurance until the house is paid off in full. Luckily, we're only a few payments away, so in a year or so, we can end our coverage."

"Legally and contractually, it sounds like that's when you have the right to do so," the Architect said tentatively. "However, I recommend you reconsider. There are plenty of benefits to having a homeowners' policy. Mortgage payment protection is only one of the benefits that come with this insurance. For example, this coverage can help protect you from the financial crisis of damages to the house? Depending on your policy, you may have financial protection from earthquakes, hurricanes, tornadoes, and more."

"I guess you're right," Robert said. He knocked on the Architect's table for effect. "We haven't had a disaster yet, so I guess we haven't given it much thought."

"Hopefully, it never happens, but it's always better to be prepared. Beyond natural disasters, homeowners' insurance provides other protection as well. For example, what if you leave the stove on and it causes a fire? Or, what if you're away on vacation, and a pipe bursts, flooding your ground floor? Homeowners' Insurance benefits you greatly in these scenarios.

"Another type of damage many homeowners' insurance policies will cover is man-made damage. For example, what if an uninsured or underinsured driver strikes your house with his car? Extensive damages could potentially cost far more than what the driver can afford. Of course, you can always sue the driver, but if they have no reserve funds, you may never see a dime. If they do have money, many judges may order them to make restitution payments, allowing them to repay you in small increments over a designated period. The problem is you may still be on the hook for those structural damages right away. A homeowners' policy could help minimize or even eradicate those costs, so you're not paying out of pocket while waiting for a reimbursement. In many cases, the insurance carrier will also take on the responsibility of recouping the costs from the driver themselves, so you don't have to deal with the legal process either."

"That's interesting," Jenny said. "I hadn't considered that. I suppose those scenarios don't happen too often, though."

"Perhaps not," the Architect continued. "Still, I hope you'll allow me to share another benefit of homeowners' insurance. Tom and Lisa are friends of yours, yes?"

"Yes," Jenny said. "In fact, we were just over at their home for a barbecue, celebrating Tom's retirement when they recommended your services."

"Great," the Architect said. "Have you ever had them over to your house for a barbecue?"

"Sure," Robert confirmed. "All the time."

"Well, I want you to imagine throwing a barbecue dinner in your backyard," the Architect said. "Let's say Tom is a bit clumsy that evening, and he trips in your backyard, falling and hitting his head on the concrete, seriously injuring himself in the process. What happens if he decides to sue you, and the court takes his side? You would be on the hook for those medical costs as they add up."

"Tom and Lisa would never do that," Jenny scoffed, "and if we truly were in the wrong, of course we'd help pay for his medical care."

"It doesn't matter," the Architect said. "Once he begins speaking with his insurance, they'll simply ask how and where he was injured. After that, the insurance company will pursue the money. What if the injured party isn't a close friend? He could be a neighborhood acquaintance or an old friend you haven't seen in years. What if a neighborhood kid decides to take a shortcut through your backyard? It wouldn't matter that he was wrong to jump that fence, you'd still likely be responsible for his care should something happen. It's better to have a policy with this particular coverage, so you don't have to worry about a simple accident threatening your nest egg."

"Yes, I suppose it is," Robert said. "We probably want to keep that policy after all. Sounds like it could come in handy should something happen. You've given us something to think about."

"Great idea," the Architect said. "Remember, it's important to seriously consider every possibility before getting rid of that protection."

"That makes perfect sense to me," Jenny said, nodding emphatically.

"While homeowners' insurance can be optional," the Architect said, "having an insurance policy on your vehicle is required by law."

"We're familiar with car insurance," Robert said. "We've both had cars since we were teenagers."

"Although, if I'm honest, I think we're a bit better at driving now than we were back then," Jenny chimed in, giggling. "At least I am."

"I would hope so!" the Architect said, laughing with her. "Let's discuss some lesser-known car insurance options you may not have considered before. When insuring cars, people don't often expect an accident, so they usually plan for small occurrences like a minor fender bender with minimal damage to both vehicles. However, what if something more serious occurs?"

"Are we in for another story?" Robert asked, smiling.

"You're learning quickly," the Architect remarked with a grin. "I knew a man—let's call him Jerry. He carried liability insurance, and he went so far as to pay a higher premium to get a higher maximum benefit. His policy even included some additional coverage to help offset the costs to his own vehicle and medical costs as well. He wanted to be prepared, and he fleshed out his auto insurance. Just in case."

"I don't like where I think this story is headed," Jenny interjected.

"Nor should you," the Architect responded, continuing. "Only three years from retirement, Jerry was driving home from the office after a long, stressful day at work. His thoughts were elsewhere, and he forgot to check his blind spot before switching lanes. He collided with another car. The accident was profoundly serious, and both drivers were rushed to the emergency room."

"Oh dear," Jenny said, covering her mouth.

"When both men were out of immediate medical danger, the police questioned Jerry and the other driver so they could file a report, which was then sent to their respective insurance companies. Jerry's auto insurance was robust, but sadly, not strong enough for this devastating blow. You see, because the other driver's car was higher value, Jerry's insurance could only cover some of the cost. The medical bills for both men were so expensive that only a portion was covered by insurance. On top of that, the other driver was paralyzed from the waist down, and he was confined to a wheelchair. The paralyzed man was ten years from his own retirement and was unable to work. Unfortunately for Jerry, the man was also a higher earner, bringing in six figures a year in income."

"What happened?" Jenny asked, apprehensively.

"As you can probably guess, the other driver sued Jerry for ten years' worth of income. Because Jerry was at fault, the man was awarded $1,000,000 to cover the loss of his income. Jerry's auto insurance was already tapped out at its maximum payouts, so Jerry was on the hook for the majority of the $1,000,000. So where do you think that money came from?"

"Oh no," Robert said. "He had to delay his retirement, didn't he?"

"That's right," the Architect continued. "Jerry had to make payments to the other man directly out of his investments. Before the accident, my friend Jerry was so close to retirement. Afterwards, because he didn't earn as much as the other driver, he was forced to work several more years before retiring himself. Even then, he didn't maintain the quality of life he'd originally planned to have due to the massive hit to his retirement nest egg."

"Wow," Jenny said, "that's scary. Just one mistake, one bad day, ended up costing both of those men so much. It sounds like Jerry was very well protected with his auto insurance, but still shouldered so much of the burden. Even with additional coverage, how would we protect ourselves against something like that?"

"Auto insurance coverage may not provide protection against such extensive damage," the Architect said, "but what if there was another way to protect yourself from paying those costs out of pocket?"

"Like what?" Robert asked, leaning in.

"Umbrella insurance," the Architect said.

"What's that?" Jenny asked, interested.

"Umbrella Insurance is a catch-all, hence the name 'Umbrella', and it's meant exactly for these types of situations. If an accident occurs, whether at home or while driving, Umbrella Insurance is designed to cover any amount above and beyond your other policies' coverage. Keep in mind, you will likely need to meet a minimum coverage requirement to qualify for an umbrella policy."

"That sounds really great, but what's the catch?" Robert said, shaking his head. "The last thing we need is another insurance policy to pay for."

"It's actually quite affordable and can protect you from financial disasters like the one I just shared with you," the

Architect said. "The average umbrella policy with a coverage of $1,000,000 can cost between $150 and $300 per year.[7] Of course, nothing could truly alleviate the permanent injuries for these men, but removing the financial stress could have been a lifesaver. The choice is yours, but I'd say the cost is usually worth the peace of mind."

"I'm inclined to agree. Again, you've given us a lot to think about," Jenny said.

"That's what I'm here for," the Architect said, sketching the final cornerstone on the blueprint. As he did so, a familiar rumble shook the ground. Eagerly they watched as the final cornerstone materialized in the final corner of the building.

"We're really making some progress now, aren't we?" Robert asked, admiring the forming foundation.

"We are," the Architect confirmed. "Now, we must fill in the space between these cornerstones with your Financial House's Foundation."

"We're ready," Jenny said.

"Then let's get started," the Architect replied, smiling.

---

[7] Sarah Schlichter. nerdwallet. September 20, 2021. "What Is Umbrella Insurance, and How Does It Work?"
https://www.nerdwallet.com/article/insurance/umbrella-insurance

Summary

- Home insurance can potentially protect you from the devastating costs of disasters like fires and floods.
- Home insurance can also offset legal costs should someone be injured on your property.
- While auto insurance is legally required, additional coverage may be a more protective choice.
- Umbrella insurance is designed to help cover any damages, medical costs, and other costs that climb above the coverage offered by your home and auto insurance policies.

Questions to Consider

1. Does your homeowners' insurance offer coverage for natural disasters that occur most often in your area, as well as isolated home disasters such as fire or floods?

____

2. Do you have the bare minimum coverage for your auto insurance, or do you have additional coverage?

____

3. If you are found at fault in an accident, are you aware of your legal liability? Will your current insurance be sufficient to cover the accident?

____

____

4. Do you understand the benefits of umbrella insurance and the financial protection an umbrella policy can offer?

____

____

Notes

THE FOUNDATION

Chapter Seven

ABOVE GROUND

Te Architect took Jenny and Robert around the perimeter of the foundation to review the construction. When he was satisfied, he spoke to the couple.

"I want to congratulate you on the progress you've made thus far. The four cornerstones support the foundation by offering financial protection against the unforeseen expenses that can pop up in our lives. Your Foundation serves a similar purpose: offering you **emotional protection**."

"I'm on board already," Jenny said. "We could certainly use some emotional protection. Whenever we talk about retirement, our stress levels skyrocket."

"That's unfortunate," the Architect said. "Dreams and plans for retirement should conjure up feelings of joy, relaxation, and contentment. Never stress."

"We would love that," Jenny said.

"Before we get started," the Architect said, "can you tell me the purpose of a house's foundation?"

"Um…to keep your house above ground," Robert said, laughing.

"You laugh, but you're absolutely right," the Architect replied with a smile. "That's one important function: it withstands the Earth's movements keeping your house, as you said, above ground. A foundation also prevents moisture from seeping into the house, and it serves as insulation. A solid foundation can potentially last forever even under the greatest of stressors."

Jenny nodded. "That's interesting. I didn't know that. How does that correlate with our Financial House?"

"I'm glad you asked," the Architect said. "Your Financial Foundation is designed with the same purpose in mind—to keep your finances above ground. It 'insulates' your nest egg, if you will, prevents leaks from getting out, and withstands the movements of the economy. Your foundation is essentially an income plan you can't outlive."

"That we can't outlive?" Robert asked, clarifying.

"When you think about your retirement, what is your biggest concern?" the Architect asked.

"Oh, that's an easy one," he replied. "I'm concerned about running out of money during our retirement. That's why we're so nervous to retire."

"I hear that concern a lot," the Architect said, "but if you'll allow me, I'd like to make just one small amendment. Instead of saying running out of *money*, I'd like you to think in terms of running out of *income*."

"What's the difference?" Jenny asked, confused.

"While you're working," the Architect said, "you receive a steady paycheck. Let's say an emergency expense comes up suddenly. You may be able to cover that cost with your current paycheck. Once that paycheck is spent, you may have to tighten your belt for a couple weeks, but at least you know that another paycheck is coming soon. When you tighten your belt for those two weeks, that's called running out of money.

"Now, what would happen if you were to quit, get laid off, or get fired from your job? You may have savings set aside, but once that savings is depleted, it's gone. There's no more cushiony paycheck just around the corner. That's running out of income."

"That makes sense," Jenny said. "But, a new job would replace that paycheck right away, so we wouldn't really be running out of income."

"You'd be absolutely right," the Architect said, "if we were still talking about your working years. However, we're talking about your retirement years. Certainly, retirement isn't an ideal time to go back to the workforce. Wouldn't you rather have a plan set up that ensures you don't outlive your income, no matter what?"

"Definitely the income plan," Jenny replied. "I see your point. So how do we do that?"

"Another great question Jenny," the Architect said. "In retirement, you have two types of income. The first is what we'll call your 'paycheck.' Your 'paycheck' is the income that covers your basic expenses, needs, and financial obligations. In other words, how much do you need to maintain your current lifestyle? What income do you require to be able to cover your groceries, utilities, insurances, and any other bills that you consider necessities? That number will be your 'paycheck.'"

"Makes sense so far," Jenny agreed.

"The second type of income, we'll call your 'play-check,'" the Architect said with a smirk.

"I like that," Jenny snickered. "Play-check."

"Your 'play-check' is the income you *want* to have to enjoy your retirement years to the fullest. For instance, if your 'paycheck' provides for your necessities, your 'play-check' provides for your luxuries. That includes golfing, cruises, road trips, gift money for spoiling the kids and grandkids, shopping money, etc. All the things you both mentioned when I asked about your retirement dreams."

"I like the sound of that," Robert said. "So, we're talking about a minimalistic budget and an enjoyment budget?"

"That's a great way to put it," the Architect said. "Remember, however, that your income needs may change in retirement. Some expenses may increase while others decrease. That's why it's important to estimate those amounts now and adjust as needed."

"It probably won't change too much, though, right?" Jenny asked, looking first at her husband, then back at the Architect.

"Only you can predict that," the Architect said, "but allow me to share a story with you that may change your mind. A few years ago, I met with a couple very much like you. They were a fun-loving couple, primed and ready to retire just like you, but they didn't have any reservations and were ready to just jump into enjoying their retirement years."

"Sounds nice," Jenny said. "I wish we had that confidence."

"In their case," the Architect continued, "that confidence could have pushed them into a small mistake that would have affected their entire lifestyle. We discussed their income plan and their need for 'paycheck' income and 'play-check' income. They told me their 'paycheck' would only need to be $4,000 per month. After reviewing their lifestyle and income with them, I felt something was off, so I asked them to take some time to review their expenses, just to be sure. They were hesitant to heed my advice. After a few eye rolls, they promised they would review their finances and get back to me."

"What did they find?" Robert asked.

"When we sat down together again the following week," the Architect said, "the husband told me quite sheepishly that he'd been mistaken, and they would need closer to $5,000 per month to live comfortably. Imagine what could have happened had they gone ahead with their initial plan. They may not have been quite as comfortable during their retirement as they'd hoped."

"I guess we better review our 'paycheck' needs as well," Jenny said, nudging her husband. "How can we estimate what we'll spend in retirement, though?"

"Well, consider this," the Architect said, "right now, approximately one-third of your life revolves around work. Currently, you may be spending more on work clothes, more on eating out if you don't take lunch to work, and more on gas for your commute."

"That's true," Jenny said.

"However," the Architect continued, "in retirement, those expenses could change. How will your life and spending habits change when you've freed up an additional forty hours every week? You might spend less on clothing because you don't need those work clothes anymore. Maybe you'll spend less on fuel once you don't have a commute, or more because you have more time for errands around town. You may stay in for meals so that cost is reduced, or maybe you'll enjoy eating out more as a couple. These are all factors to consider when designing your income plan."

The couple nodded.

"And those are only predictable expenses," the Architect said. "What about factors you can't control—like your health? As we get older, our bodies inevitably begin to break down, regardless of your current health or how well you take care of yourself. That means your healthcare costs could potentially increase, as we discussed with our second cornerstone conversation."

"Something to think about," Jenny said. "We'll consider our health as we create our budget."

"Do you see how critical your income plan is for retirement?" the Architect asked. "Without a proper income plan, if the worst were to happen, you could potentially run out of income before you expected. With an income plan that provides for your basic needs, you never have to worry about that again. Even if you lost a large portion of your money in the markets, you know your basic income is still providing for your needs. It may mean less of what you want to do, but at least you'll have enough to support yourselves."

"Yikes, could we really lose that much? Is that very likely to happen?"

"The economy is always changing and evolving," the Architect said. "I'm sure you remember the terrible recession our economy suffered from late 2007 through early 2009. More recently, the continual effects from the COVID-19 virus may permanently change the way our economy functions. We've seen what these events could do to our country and our investments. We know these things happen from time to time. I'd love to be able to tell you that the economy will never again see a recession, but that would be naïve. That's why I believe it's so important to build your foundation first. We *hope* for the best, but we *plan* for the worst."

"Better safe than sorry," Robert said, agreeing.

"That's right," the Architect said. "If you've created an income plan you can't outlive, then you know you're going to be okay financially. No matter how the market performs, no matter what's going on in the economy, even if we're in a low-interest rate environment, your planned income will cover your basic needs."

"So how do we create this income plan?" Robert asked.

"Yes," Jenny agreed. "How do we even begin to build our foundation? Supplying that level of income just seems so overwhelming."

"Well," the Architect replied, "you know that most investments depend on the performance of the market, so our foundation isn't built on those. In fact, I've met with many people who have been able to fund their entire foundation through other means, for example, through Social Security. Let's return to our $5,000 per month example. Robert, let's say your Social Security check is $2,000 per month. Jenny, let's say yours is $1,500. Together, that's $3,500 per month. Now, that's not the full $5,000 we believe we need to build our foundation, but, fortunately, we're two-thirds of the way there already!"

"That's true," Robert said. "I hadn't thought of Social Security as a part of our Financial House, but I guess you're right. It's a steady monthly income just like a paycheck."

"That's right," the Architect said. "Now, how do we provide the rest? Let's see. Do either of you have a pension?"

"I do," Jenny said, suddenly excited. "I work for the state."

"Wonderful," the Architect said. "Pensions are becoming a thing of the past, so if you have one to help fund your Foundation, consider yourself truly fortunate. Now, let's imagine those pension benefits add another $1,000 to your foundation," the Architect said. "Now, you have a grand total of $4,500 per month. We've made some great progress. However, we're still short by $500 per month. So, let's take a look at what we can do to fill in that gap."

"For example, let's imagine a couple, both aged sixty-five, are short $500 per month, or $6,000 per year. This couple has $50,000 in their savings account as a cushion for their Cash Reserves Cornerstone. We don't want to touch that if we don't have to, but it's important to keep it in mind. Now, let's look at investments. Let's say you have $500,000 in investments.

"Now, according to the Social Security Administration, a male turning sixty-five in 2021 generally has a life expectancy between eighteen and nineteen more years depending on their date of birth[8], which means he's expected to live until eighty-three or eighty-four years. A sixty-five-year-old female, on the other hand, has a life expectancy between twenty and twenty-two more years, meaning she's expected to live until eighty-five or eighty-six. That means we need to plan to provide for twenty years of income." The Architect paused for a moment to think. "Actually, let's round that up to twenty-five just to be safe because you two are active and healthy. So, twenty-five years multiplied by $6,000 per year is $150,000. So, we know we can provide that by using that amount of the $500,000 in investments, filling their income gap and still leaving $350,000 in investments. This plan provides you with a four percent payout each year, creating an income of $6,000 per year. All while you still have control of your money, no matter the value of the account."

"I'm concerned about planning for just twenty-five years, though," Jenny said. "People are living longer these days. What happens if we outlive that $150,000?"

"That's a great question," the Architect replied. "Keep in mind that the example I just shared with you is only the base number. We haven't taken interest or returns into account. The types of investments we will likely consider usually provide somewhere between three and five percent in returns every year on average. That growth can potentially last much longer than the initial twenty-five years.

"That said, if you're worried about that, you may have to make a decision for yourselves in this potential scenario. Do you settle for the $350,000 in investments, or do you adjust your lifestyle needs? You can adjust up or down to suit your comfort level as well as your lifestyle, but as you can see,

---

[8] https://www.ssa.gov/oact/population/longevity.html

making up that difference is entirely possible with the right planning."

"But didn't you say our investments depend on the market?" Robert asked. "Doesn't that mean that the income isn't a sure thing?'

"It's true," the Architect said. "If you can avoid using investments, that's the best-case scenario. Many people don't need to use their investments at all. Sometimes, Social Security and pension payouts can make up the foundation together, depending on your lifestyle needs and basic living expenses. However, suppose there is a difference between what you need and what your Social Security and pension can provide. In that case, there are a few strategies to ensure your investable assets can become part of a strong foundation as long as you're choosing the right option for you and your situation."

"Right," Jenny said. "So, couldn't we just leave our investments where they are, and still use them as income?"

"The key to a solid foundation is ensuring you always have your basic living expenses covered with a solid income plan you can't outlive. You're certainly welcome to leave your investments where they are and plan on withdrawing a certain percentage each year to provide your income. But what would happen if the market went through a recession like the one we faced from 2007 to 2009? You could lose thirty, maybe even forty percent, and find yourselves unable to maintain your lifestyle without running out of money. It's far better to be confident that your basic needs will always be met regardless of the changing market. We build the foundation outside of your investments because we want you to be able to protect your principal. The foundation needs to be income you can't lose.

"Of course, you'll still have the $350,000 in investments to augment your lifestyle so you can enjoy your retirement all the more."

"We'll certainly bear that in mind," Robert said.

"The purpose of your foundation," the Architect said, "is to provide you with **Emotional Protection.** It's designed to remove the financial worry from your everyday life. With a solid foundation, you never need to worry about outliving your money. Instead, your only worry should be where you want to go on your next vacation."

"That's great news," Jenny said, smiling.

The Architect gestured for Robert and Jenny to step away from the construction site. "You two may want to step back for this next part." Robert and Jenny quickly backed up as the earth rumbled even more heavily. Astounded, they watched the full foundation settle into place.

"A beautiful sight indeed," the Architect sighed.

Summary

- Before you retire, define your current expenses. Compare that budget to your expected basic income needs once you retire. Your income plan will most likely change.
- In retirement, you have two purposes for your money—your paycheck and your play-check.
- Your foundation is designed to offer emotional protection, meaning you don't have to worry about your income unexpectedly running out.
- Social Security and pension benefits will often be able to make up most or all your foundation.

Questions to Consider

1. Have you considered the amount you'll need for your monthly expenses to build a solid foundation?

____

2. How much of your basic living expenses could be covered by your Social Security check?

____

3. Do you have a pension? If so, will those benefits, when added to Social Security, make up the entirety of your Financial Foundation to provide you with an income plan you can't outlive?

____

4. What amount, if any, will you need to reallocate from your investments to help you create a lifetime income source? Does this source account for the difference between your Social Security and pension benefits, and your basic living expenses?

____

____

Notes

THE WALLS

Chapter Nine

KEEPING THE FUTURE IN MIND

"**B**efore we continue," the Architect said, "I want you to take a moment and admire the progress you've made so far," the Architect said, gesturing to their construction site. You have constructed four cornerstones and built yourselves a solid foundation. That means no matter what happens from this point on, you can have financial peace of mind. To review, your cornerstones are designed to create Asset Protection for your home, your cars, and, most importantly, your health and your lives. Your foundation provides you with Emotional Protection, giving you peace of mind as the markets and economy change all around you because you have an income plan you can't outlive that isn't affected by economic changes."

"Looking at the big picture," Jenny said, "does give me a sense of peace."

"I'm glad," the Architect said. "Now that we know what the cornerstones and foundation are designed to do, let's talk about your walls. You said yourselves that you don't want to just survive your retirement years, you want to live those years to the fullest, to enjoy them."

"You're right," Robert said. "We want to take advantage of every moment we have together."

"We'll finally have time to travel," Jenny pitched in. "I'd love to see our family more often than we've been able to while we've been working. Not to mention taking some of those dream vacations."

"Wonderful goals to be sure," the Architect said. "After all, you've spent most of your lives working hard to get to this point. You've earned a respite from the world of work. Your Walls are designed to offer you a new type of protection - **Principal Protection.**"

"Wait," Jenny said, "doesn't our foundation protect our principal?"

"That's true," the Architect said. "Technically, both the foundation and walls protect your principal. Where your Foundation provides the income you can't outlive, your Walls are investments that are also principal protected and still maintain a steady level of growth.

"In retirement, it's important to shift your perspective regarding your investments. When you're young and first starting out, your investment goals are primarily to accumulate growth that you can hopefully use in retirement. You don't worry too much about minor losses based on your risk tolerance because you have the time to make up for those losses over time."

"That's true. We've taken that approach most of our lives," Robert agreed.

"Have you heard the phrase 'only a paper loss?'" the Architect asked.

"Of course," Jenny said.

"Well," the Architect continued, "early in your career, the 'paper loss' metaphor is usually true. Generally, when you don't need to withdraw the money from your investments, your losses will most likely be made up over time. Of course, there's never a guarantee, but the market tends to trend upward in the long run, therefore investments generally see growth over time.

"Once you're preparing to retire, you may no longer have years and years to make up 'paper losses' so it could become an actual loss. Five to ten years before you retire, change your mindset regarding your investments. It's time to shift your focus from accumulation and growth of your wealth to the preservation of said wealth. Some couples I've met with have already retired but haven't shifted their investment mindsets. If they haven't already, I encourage them to make the same shift. Better late than never."

"Okay," Jenny said. "I'd never thought of it that way before, but that makes sense."

"Remember," the Architect added, "some of your investment money has been repurposed to become a part of your income plan to supplement your Social Security and pension checks. Your walls will also use a portion of your investment money, but this segment will serve to keep pace with inflation, or, as I like to call it, Inflation Insurance. The money invested in your walls still has conservative growth potential, but without the risk associated with investing in the fluctuating market."

"So, what exactly are these principal-protected investments?" Robert asked.

"There are several types of accounts," the Architect said, thoughtfully, "many of which you'll recognize. We're talking about the types of accounts offered by banks—savings, checking, money markets, etc. Of course, while these accounts carry minimal to no risk, you'll also reap minimal interest and growth."

"You're not kidding," Robert said. "Interest rates are so low for banks these days. I remember back in the eighties, I was getting fifteen percent interest on some of my accounts."

"We were still getting five or six percent in the nineties," Jenny pitched in. "Times sure have changed."

"They certainly have," the Architect concurred. "And that's why these types of accounts are currently being used primarily in your Cash Reserves Cornerstone. As rates rise or fall, you can always review and determine whether these types of accounts belong in the construction of your Walls, since you still want to have some growth. Some of the most powerful retirement accounts that can be invested in your Walls are IRAs, 401(k)s, and similar accounts, including Roth IRAs and Roth 401(k)s. We'll get a little deeper into those types of accounts later. We can also use non-retirement accounts such as CDs, annuities, or government bonds."

"Okay," Jenny said.

"There's one in particular that I'd like to talk about in detail: CDs, or Certificates of Deposit. These accounts generally offer a higher rate of return than your standard checking and savings accounts, but there's a catch. You'll need to commit to having your money tied up for a predetermined amount of time. Generally, you'll see timeframes anywhere from thirty days to five years. In most cases, the longer you agree to keep your money in the account, the higher the interest rate you'll receive."

"But what if an emergency pops up?" Jenny asked. "I know our Cash Reserves Cornerstone covers that, but what if our emergency fund isn't enough to cover an expense? Would we be charged a surrender fee to pull our money out of the CD early?"

The Architect scratched his chin as he thought. "Well, yes and no. Generally, most CDs will place a penalty on the CD instead of charging an early withdrawal fee. If you withdraw your money earlier than the maturity date or arrangement date, you may have to surrender a designated amount of your interest based on the length of the CD investment. For a one-year CD, you may have to surrender three months' interest. For longer CDs, depending on the arrangement, you may need to surrender six months to one year's interest. Every bank has its own terms, though, so make sure you double-check with your bank to see what their CD surrender policy is before you make a decision."

"We'd definitely have to plan on not touching that money, even in emergencies. So, is the principal in these investments always protected?" Jenny asked.

"Well," the Architect said, "I tend to avoid absolutes like 'always.' 'Always' implies that nothing can change, and we know that's not true. However, CD accounts have a vast history of principal protection to fall back on. Let's go all the way back to the Great Depression. Many banks were failing. After the Depression ended in 1933, a new organization to help ensure financial institutions was founded, the Federal Deposit Insurance Corporation. You've most likely seen their initials everywhere in your bank—FDIC."

"Oh yes," Jenny confirmed. "I have seen those little FDIC plaques at our bank, so that makes me feel better."

"If your money is in the bank, it's insured by the FDIC up to $250,000. This insurance exists to offer people a sense of security when they invest their money in a bank. They feel safe, knowing that even if the bank fails, they'll get up to $250,000 of their hard-earned money back."

"Some of our money is in a credit union as well," Robert added. "Does the FDIC also guarantee that money?"

"Actually" the Architect replied, "if you're using a credit union instead of a bank, your money is insured by a separate organization called the National Credit Union Association, or NCUA. Most credit unions use the NCUA to insure their members' money, again up to $250,000. If a credit union chooses to be state chartered rather than federally chartered, they may instead be insured by private deposit insurance. If you're curious about how the money in your credit union is insured, make time to sit down with your financial institution to find out."

"Makes sense," Jenny said. "So, I know we shouldn't keep more than a year's income in our bank for cash reserves. But just out of curiosity, what would happen if we had more than $250,000 in the bank?"

"As long as your bank remains in good standing, that money would continue to grow at the interest rate the bank advertised. However, if your bank were to fall on hard times, any amount above $250,000 could potentially be lost."

"Well, that's the reason not to keep too much in the bank, I suppose," Jenny said. "Not that we would, but it's always interesting to learn what could happen."

"I agree," the Architect said. "Now, one more option I'd like to discuss with you is annuities. Before you react, I'm fully aware that annuities are a polarizing topic. Based on your life experience or what you've read or heard in the media, you may have a predetermined opinion of them - you either love them or hate them. The truth is they're just like any other investment—there are pros and cons. If you have concerns, do your research, and take the time to weigh your options to see what type of account or investment works best for you. Never make a decision based on something you've read online or seen on the news. Everyone's situation is unique and what's right for you may not be right for someone else, and vice versa."

"Right," Robert said. "So, keep an open mind. I can do that."

"Great," the Architect said. "Let's discuss how annuities work."

"Okay," Jenny said.

"Annuities are an investment vehicle generally offered by insurance companies. Because insurance companies have their own financial laws, these accounts are guaranteed by reserve accounts, instead of the FDIC or NCUA. There are four types of annuities, and we're going to discuss a couple of them."

"Okay," Rob said.

"The first two types of annuities are the Immediate Annuity and the Variable Annuity," the Architect said. "These are generally the ones people tend to like less. Because these types of annuities aren't investment vehicles designed for building your walls, we're not going to talk about them today."

"I see," Robert said. "So, are there types of annuities that do work to help build our walls?

"That's a great question," the Architect said, "These next two annuity types can be part of your walls. The first one is a Fixed Annuity. Much like CDs, a Fixed Annuity generally locks your investment in for a predetermined amount of time in exchange for a higher interest rate. The terms can range between one to five years, but you might see some with longer terms. Typically, the longer-term commitment you make, the higher interest rate you'll receive at the end of the investment. Also, while every bank and insurance company vary, historically, fixed annuities tend to offer a slightly higher rate of return than CDs."

"The final type of annuity I want to discuss with you is the Fixed Index Annuity," the Architect said. "The money you invest into an annuity increases in value based on the state of the market. You agree to accept a percentage of the upside of the gains, while taking no losses from the downside. This gives you the potential for growth without the regular risk you'd be taking if you were fully invested in the market. For example, if the market is up ten percent, you may potentially see anywhere from four to seven percent of that upside. If the market's up twenty percent, you may see anywhere from eight to fourteen percent. If the market's down, you'll see zero gains and zero losses. I want to say that again to make sure you understand the value here—you can't lose money due to dips in the market."

"Wow," Jenny said. "That really sounds impressive."

"An additional benefit of choosing to invest in an annuity," the Architect continued, "is the liquidity. Many options allow you to withdraw certain amounts annually. either your earnings or up to ten percent annually. You can either withdraw the interest you earned on the account, or possibly even a portion of the investment itself, sometimes up to ten percent annually, without penalty. Remember, most annuities have several liquidity options and terms can vary, so make sure you discuss the particulars with your Financial Architect and understand the details before you take any action."

"Of course," Jenny said, nodding, "I'm definitely interested in looking into those options further."

"Another investment option you may consider," the Architect continued, "is government savings bonds. These investments are backed by the government, which many people may feel is an advantage over other options. These accounts are assigned interest upon your initial investment. That interest at full value is only guaranteed after the maturity of the bond. Between your initial investment and that maturity date, the interest you would receive should you withdraw early would be based upon the length of the investment and how early you are taking your money."

"Good to know," Robert said. "In other words, we wouldn't want to pull out the money early if we can help it."

"That's right," the Architect said. "Another similar option is U.S. treasury notes and bonds, which are also principal protected and backed by the U.S. government. One thing to remember here is that should you attempt to sell your U.S. treasury bonds before their maturity date, you may lose a portion of your principal, so I recommend holding them until full-term."

"Thanks," Jenny said.

"Now that you understand how your walls work, let's take a moment to review what they're designed to do. The first job for your Walls is setting off inflation. Historical inflation has grown an average of three percent per year. While many recent years have seen a slightly smaller increase, it's best to count on that three percent average. History doesn't guarantee the future, but it does give us an idea of where to start when we make our retirement plan. The gains you see from your walls most likely won't be as overly impressive, but they may help you keep pace with inflation."

"Okay," Robert said.

"Secondly," the Architect continued, "the Walls provide a lifestyle income cushion. Remember that your Foundation provides you with all your basic needs, so you know you'll be okay no matter what happens. Well, the Walls are designed to increase your quality of life. Think of all those extra hobbies you're looking forward to - traveling, golfing, spoiling the grandkids, and so much more. Your Walls are designed to earn an average return of 3 to 6 percent over a five-to-ten-year period," the Architect said. "With strong, inflation-resistant Walls, you'll accomplish quite a lot with your hard-earned money, so you can really enjoy your retirement years."

"Now there's an idea I can jump on board with," Jenny said. "Let's get those walls built."

"That's the spirit!" the Architect exclaimed. "And you have a lot of freedom in your building strategies. Based on what's happening in the economy at any given time, you could use all the options we've discussed, or just a few at a time."

He smiled as he turned his attention to the concrete foundation they were standing on. Rob knew that look by now, and he impulsively grabbed Jenny's hand as the earth shook. In just a few moments, tall thick walls seemed to sprout right out of the ground, reaching a two-story height before ceasing to grow. "Wow," Jenny breathed, in awe of the amazing sight. Their work so far had been magical, and they looked forward to learning what came next as they finished their Financial House.

Summary

- Your walls are designed to provide principal protection and potentially offset inflation.
- CDs, government savings bonds, government treasuries, and annuities are several types of investments you will need to protect your principal.
- Plan on seeing an average return of 3 to 6 percent over five to ten years.
- A solid portion of your investments should be in the investment options that make up the walls.
- Depending on the ever-changing economy, you may choose to use one or two of these options at a time, or a combination of all of them.

Questions to Consider

1. Have you shifted your perspective from investment growth and accumulation to preserving your wealth?

____

____

2. As you design your retirement plan, have you considered inflation and its potential effect on your retirement income?

____

____

3. Have you considered annuities, treasuries, and/or CDs as viable investment vehicles to help offset inflation so you can continue enjoying your current lifestyle throughout retirement?

____

____

Notes

THE BEAMS

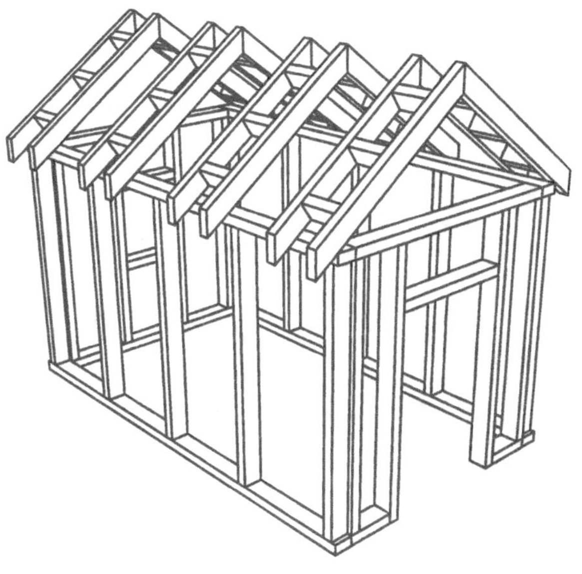

Chapter Ten

A BRIEF EXPLANATION OF TAX REDUCTION

The Architect ran his hand over the smooth finish of the wall to his right, guiding their gaze to the open sky above. "Atop our walls sits the roof," he said, "but the roof must be properly supported. To do that, we build support beams. **The Beams of your Financial House represent your tax plan.**"

"I'm not a fan of taxes," Jenny said.

"Then I'm sure you'd be happy to know taxes are lower now than they've been in a long time. In fact, taxes have been lower these past thirty years than they have been since 1931, nearly a century ago."

"No complaints there," Robert said, smiling.

"I agree. It's wonderful," the Architect replied. "However, how long will that last?"

"Hopefully forever," Jenny replied with an uncertain grin.

"I'm with you, but I'm afraid that may not be in the cards," the Architect said. "In fact, we know that our current tax rates have an expiration date. At the end of 2025, the Tax Cuts and Jobs Act expires. Unless our government extends the current rates or cuts taxes in another way, we could potentially see rates rise back to the levels before 2017 or perhaps even as high as they were in the mid-80s[9]. Here, let me show you."

The Architect guided the couple through the opening of their financial front door and back to the drafting table. He shuffled through some files beneath his blueprints until he uncovered a chart, placing the image on top for the couple to see:

---

[9] taxpolicycenter.org. February 4, 2020. "Historical Highest Marginal Income Tax Rates" https://www.taxpolicycenter.org/statistics/historical-highest-marginal-income-tax-rates

Historical Highest Tax Rates

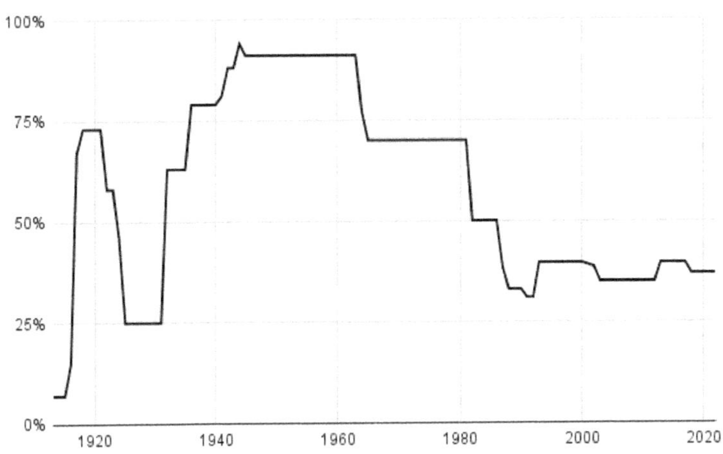

*Source: Mark Luscombe, JD, LLM, CPA. Wolters Kluwer. December 2022.
"Historical income tax rates." https://www.wolterskluwer.com/en/expert-
insights/whole-ball-of-tax-historical-income-tax-
rates#:~:text=The%20top%20income%20tax%20rate,decline%20began%2C%2
0ending%20in%201987.*

"Wow," Jenny said, examining the numbers. "I can't believe how these figures have changed. I mean I'd heard taxes were higher during the Depression and World War II, but some of these numbers are outrageous. I guess we really have been fortunate these past thirty years."

"Quite right," the Architect said. "When these current tax cuts expire, it's important for you to know where your tax bracket could potentially fall. Here's the key: knowing how placement in a higher tax bracket could affect your cash flow. You'll also need to examine the impact that would have on your retirement income, and therefore, your retirement lifestyle."

"If I had to guess, I'd say we could expect the same tax situation we had back then," Robert conjectured.

"Well, maybe not," Jenny added. "Afterall, we make quite a bit more money now than we did 30 years ago. Maybe we'd be in a higher bracket after all."

"It's worth considering," the Architect agreed. "In that vein, it's important to know which of your investments are taxable and what you could potentially alter to pay fewer, possibly even no taxes."

"No tax?" Jenny asked, incredulous. "Is that even possible?"

"With the proper planning and right circumstances, it is," said the Architect. "Have either of you heard of David M. Walker?"

"I can't say that we have," Jenny said, shaking her head. Robert agreed with a shrug.

"Well, Mr. Walker held *two* especially important positions in our nation's government from 1998 to 2008," the Architect said. "He was the Comptroller General and the head of the Government Accountability Office.[10] While he held those positions, he served under both the Clinton and Bush administrations."

"Interesting," Robert said.

"As Comptroller General," the Architect continued, "Walker worked closely with the Federal government's budget, and he started to notice some red flags. He believed the government's spending was out of control. As he put it, 'We're spending more money than we make, charging it to a credit card, and expecting our grandchildren to pay for it.'[11]

---

[10] Caroline Counoyer. governing.com. June 28, 2012. "David Walker's Plan to Fix America" https://www.governing.com/archive/david-walkers-plan-to-fix-america.html

[11] 60 Minutes episode: David Walker. July 2007. https://www.youtube.com/watch?v=U19_OkPRggE

Gross Federal Debt Over the Years

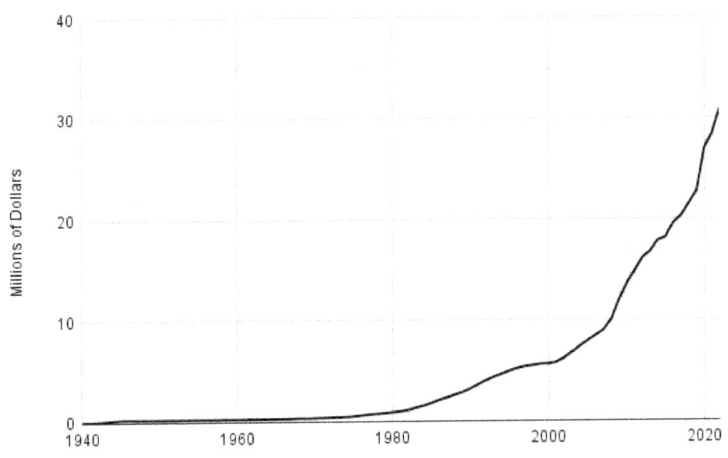

Source: The White House. "Historical Tables."
https://www.whitehouse.gov/omb/budget/historical-tables/

"That's terrible," Jenny said. "Still, what can we do? Outside of voting for the leaders that will most closely represent our values, we don't have much control over how the government spends our tax dollars."

"On a national level, you're probably right," the Architect said. "However, you can ensure they don't get more than their fair share in taxes from *you*."

"If I can do my part by keeping more of my hard-earned money, I'm in! But how do we do that?" Robert asked, curious.

The Architect laughed. "You can take this time to plan. The federal government knows their bills will eventually be called due. That means every American taxpayer will be on the hook for whatever deficit our nation has accrued. That's why it's important to review your taxes to see how you can reduce the amount you pay, including income tax, investment tax, dividends, etc."

"Sounds good," Jenny said, "but how does it work?"

"By doing the proper planning and working closely with a Financial Architect like myself, many people have been able to find themselves in a zero percent tax bracket. Those with pensions or certain types of investments may find themselves above that desired zero percent but still in a lower tax bracket than they were previously."

"I prefer zero," Jenny said, "but lower sounds good too."

"It does, doesn't it?" the Architect agreed. "Regardless of your financial situation, planning for potentially rising taxes is a critical piece of any retirement plan. If you look back through history, the last time tax rates were this low was during the Great Depression. At that time, the Federal government lowered taxes to help stimulate the struggling economy. Once our economy had recovered, the tax rates skyrocketed again. The highest tax bracket during the Great Depression was 25 percent. In 1932, however, as the Depression was coming to its end, the tax rate jumped to 63 percent."

"What a difference!" Robert exclaimed.

"By the 1940s, the top tax brackets peaked over eighty percent. In 1944 and 1945, the top tax bracket reached an all-time high of 94 percent. From 1946 through 1950, the top brackets settled down into the mid-eighties, but jumped up into the nineties again in 1951 for anyone earning $200,000 or more per year.

"Earning that kind of income back then was rarer than today, but the tax bracket still affected many, including someone you might remember, Ronald Reagan.

"I'm sure you know that before Ronald Reagan became our 40th president in 1981, he worked quite successfully as an actor. After he served in World War II in the 1940's, his acting career really took off. As he put it, he was 'making handsome money.'[12]

"In 1951, the tax rates increased to 91 percent. While Reagan continued to earn, he stated that his money 'lost a lot of its beauty and substance going through the income tax.' He once shared this anecdote. He invited several guests out to a fancy Hollywood restaurant and picked up the $200 bill. When reporting the expense to his agent, the agent informed him he'd have to earn several times that amount to pay himself back for his generosity. All because of those high tax brackets.

"Reagan didn't make more than two movies per year due to the high percentage of income lost to income tax. If he made more than $200,000, he would only keep six cents for every dollar he earned. Of course, that was before the state of California took their share as well. Needless to say, in those days, it almost seemed like earning that much money wasn't worth the effort."

"Do you think something like that could happen to taxes again?" Jenny asked nervously.

"Unfortunately, you'd need a crystal ball to make that kind of prediction," the Architect said. "All we can do is reference history and make an educated guess. While history doesn't guarantee what the future will be, it's a good idea to study the patterns of the past and go from there."

"Is there anything else you can share with us regarding taxes?" Robert asked.

"Of course," the Architect said. "Next, we'll talk about the three types of investments and how they're taxed."

---

[12] Reagan Well-Rehearsed in Tax Antagonist Role (https://www.chicagotribune.com/news/ct-xpm-1985-06-09-8502060477-story.html)

Summary

- David Walker worked for the Federal government for a decade between 1998 and 2008, serving under two presidential administrations. He believed government spending was out of control.
- The Tax Cuts and Jobs Act will expire at the end of 2025, meaning taxes will revert to their previous rates unless the Federal government enacts changes on or before that date.
- With proper planning, you can potentially lower your tax rate. Under the right circumstances, you could even possibly reach a zero percent tax bracket.

Questions to Consider

1. When the Tax Cuts and Jobs Act expires at the end of 2025, are you prepared for the rise in tax rates and brackets? Have you prepared to keep your tax rate low?

____

____

____

____

____

2. Are you working with the right Financial Architect to find ways to potentially reduce your taxes?

____

____

____

____

____

Notes

Chapter Eleven

WHAT'S HOLDING UP YOUR ROOF?

"**N**ow that we've looked at tax fluctuation and its role in your overall retirement plan," the Architect said, "I'd like to discuss how your investments are taxed. By arranging those investments properly, you can reduce or even eliminate your taxes, creating the stability for your Financial House - the Beams."

"The Beams?" Jenny asked.

"That's right," the Architect said. "While your Walls and Roof represent the investments you make, your Beams are the various ways in which your investments are taxed. With properly structured Beams, set up to reduce your taxes efficiently and accurately, you can create an even more successful retirement plan. You have three different types of investment accounts that are all taxed differently as well."

"You had me at 'reduce your taxes,'" Rob said. "What are the three?"

"The three types of investments are Taxable, Tax-Deferred, and Tax-Free," the Architect replied.

"Oh," Jenny said, "well, that's an easy one. We clearly want our money in tax-free investments."

"Now, hold on a moment," the Architect said. "While Tax-Free certainly sounds the most promising, each of these investments have their place in supporting your Financial House. A strong Financial House needs balance."

"Each of them has a place?" Jenny asked. "Even Taxable?"

"Yes, even Taxable," the Architect answered. "In fact, let's start there if you don't mind. Some examples of taxable investments are your checking and savings accounts, your stocks, bonds, dividends, real estate investments earning income, among others. If you have any of these types of accounts, you're most likely used to receiving a 1099 form at the end of each year—what I like to call a 'Thank You Note' from the IRS. That form shows how much you earned the previous year, determining what income or investments you're expected to pay tax."

"Right," Rob said, "so the idea is to get out of those accounts as much as possible, right?"

"Again," the Architect said, "each investment type has its place. Remember back to our First Cornerstone discussion on Cash Reserves? That money should be in taxable accounts, generally because taxable assets are liquid, meaning they're immediately available when you need them."

"That's true," Jenny said. "I see what you're saying."

"Remember, it's best to have three months' to one year's income available in those cash reserve accounts," the Architect continued. "In most cases, anything above that should reside in one of the other two types of tax classifications in the Tax Beams, as you mentioned. Still, it's important not to overlook the value of those cash reserves. Another reason to keep money in a taxable account is if you're saving up for a major expense—a car, a second home, or a vacation. It's good to have those long-term savings easily accessible to you when you need them."

"That makes sense," Jenny replied.

"Now, if you're not saving up for something specific or sustaining your emergency cash, why pay tax unnecessarily on that money? Even if you need the income, there are usually more tax-efficient ways to save and distribute that income. That brings us to our next category: Tax-Deferred."

"Paying taxes later sounds good to me," Jenny said.

"It does *sound* good, doesn't it?" the Architect agreed. "That's what the federal government wants you to think too."

"What do you mean?" Rob asked, leaning forward.

"Allow me to explain," the Architect said. "Have either of you heard of the Marshmallow Test?"

"I don't think so," Jenny said, shaking her head.

"Back in the 1960s," the Architect said, "Walter Mischel, a Professor of Psychology, created what he called the Marshmallow Test. The test was simple. A young child was left alone in a room with a single marshmallow on a plate. The child was told that he or she could eat the marshmallow at any time, but by waiting a short period of time, he or she could have several marshmallows instead."

"I'd like to see our grandkids wait even two minutes," Robert said, chuckling. "I'd bet they couldn't do it. Especially the younger ones."

The Architect laughed. "As you've pointed out, the study was originally designed to show the draw of instant gratification. The test taught us that the children who were able to delay their gratification with the marshmallow were also more likely to do better in school, have higher self-esteem, and were even less likely to be overweight thirty years later. It seemed like a fun little test about a child's willpower, but the results proved quite useful."

"It's an interesting study," Jenny said, "but what does it have to do with tax-deferred accounts? I'm guessing we're the children who were able to delay gratification because we put our money into IRAs to let it grow?"

"Well," the Architect replied, "you're actually not the children in this example. You're the researchers supplying the marshmallows. The IRS represents the children in this example, and they have adopted a delayed gratification mindset. They know that if they allow you to put off paying tax on your one marshmallow, or your IRA investment, they can get the tax on all the growth and interest your marshmallows have accrued when it finally comes time to collect. They know their patience will pay off in the long run."

"Wow," Rob said, "I never thought of it like that."

"Another way I like to explain it," the Architect continued, "is from the point of view of a farmer. Would you rather pay tax on the seeds or the crops that grow from those seeds? Tax-deferral doesn't sound so appealing anymore, does it?"

"I'd rather pay the tax on the small seeds instead of the large crops for sure," Rob added.

"That's right," the Architect said. "We're encouraged to set up IRAs when we're young for a reason. We buy into it because we believe we'll have more money to pay that tax in the future, and maybe the tax brackets will get reduced as well. We also start believing the myth that we'll retire in a lower tax bracket, but that's usually not true for those who have saved and invested properly."

"That's true," Jenny said.

"Also," the Architect continued, "remember that tax brackets have been lower these past thirty years than they've been since the Great Depression. The odds of them dipping down even further are quite unlikely, especially when you look at the state of our economy these past few years.

"Sometimes we forget this aspect too. When we're young and working, we can claim more credits and deductions on our taxes, such as children, that you might not be able to claim when you retire. You may even, heaven forbid, be widowed by that point, and be left paying taxes as a single taxpayer again."

"I guess we were bamboozled by the old snake oil salesman," Jenny said. "I can't believe we fell for that!"

"Don't be too hard on yourselves," the Architect said. "Almost everyone did. In fact, around 75 percent of the people I visit with on a regular basis bought into this bill of goods only to later discover they'd lit the fuse on a tax time bomb."

"You're not kidding," Jenny said.

"That bomb goes off when you reach age seventy-two," the Architect continued, "because whether you need the money or not, you're required to withdraw a percentage of that money every year after that point."

"Oh yes, those are the RMDs right?" Robert conjectured.

"Required Minimum Distributions," the Architect clarified. "You see, when you invest in an IRA, 401(k), or another type of tax-deferred account, you are essentially taking on a partner over your assets. You're giving up full control of your money."

"Now hang on a minute," Jenny said. "We *do* have a couple IRAs, but that's still our money in there."

"You're right. It is," the Architect said, "but the IRS is your senior partner in a sense. They control when you're *allowed* and *required* to withdraw that money, and even *how much* you're required to withdraw."

The Architect rummaged through a few more papers at the table and pulled out a smaller sheet of paper. "In fact, this chart shows you exactly what your requirements are."

To Calculate RMD: Divide the December 31 account value by the factor that corresponds to your age: December 31 value/factor = RMD

Based on IRS Table III: Uniform Lifetime Table

For Use by:

- *Unmarried Owners,*

- *Married Owners Whose Spouses Aren't More Than 10 Years Younger, and*

- *Married Owners Whose Spouses Aren't the Sole Beneficiaries of Their IRAs*

Age	Distribution Period	Age	Distribution Period
73	26.5	97	7.8
74	25.5	98	7.3
75	24.6	99	6.8
76	23.7	100	6.4
77	22.9	101	6.0
78	22.0	102	5.6
79	21.1	103	5.2
80	20.2	104	4.9
81	19.4	105	4.6
82	18.5	106	4.3
83	17.7	107	4.1
84	16.8	108	3.9
85	16.0	109	3.7
86	15.2	110	3.5
87	14.4	111	3.4
88	13.7	112	3.3
89	12.9	113	3.1
90	12.2	114	3.0
91	11.5	115	2.9
92	10.8	116	2.8
93	10.1	117	2.7
94	9.5	118	2.5
95	8.9	119	2.3
96	8.4	120+	2.0

"Wow," Jenny said, looking over at her husband. "We really did hand over the control, didn't we?"

"I think we blew it," Robert said, nodding solemnly.

"Now, remember," the Architect emphasized, "you can accomplish many things financially with proper planning. It's not good or bad, per se, to invest money in an IRA, 401(k), 403(b), or other tax-deferred accounts. However, it's important to know what you're signing up for, and how it can potentially affect the taxes you'll pay on that income in retirement."

"It's too late for that, I'd say," Robert said, shaking his head.

"It's never too late," the Architect disagreed. "Even though you have money in a tax-deferred account, you can strategically withdraw your money from your IRA in a tax-efficient way that potentially enables you to pay fewer taxes and potentially no tax on some of that money in the long run. How, when, and why you withdraw that money all play a part of the planning process. That's why it's important to work with a Financial Architect like myself to discover what options are available to you."

"Like what?" Jenny asked.

"Well," the Architect said, "let me ask you this: Do you donate to charity?"

"We do," Robert replied. "We have a couple causes we care deeply about, and we give frequently to our church."

"Great," the Architect said. "Starting at age seventy-two, instead of writing a check to the charity of your choice, you can arrange for your RMDs, or a portion of them, to be donated to charity rather than withdrawing them to be used as income. By donating from this account, you transform this tax-deferred account into a tax-free one. And, you'll still be donating to the causes or the church you were already supporting. And that's just one of the options."

"Are there any others?" Jenny asked, intrigued.

"That question leads us to my personal favorite of the tax beams - the Tax-Free Beam."

"I like the sound of that one," Robert said.

"I thought you might," the Architect said. "Once you realize the control the IRS has over your IRA money, knowing what control *you* have becomes increasingly important. So, you have a decision to make."

"What decision?" Robert asked.

"When do you want to take back control of your money?" the Architect asked.

"How about right now?" Robert suggested, "or at least as soon as possible."

"That's a great answer," the Architect replied. "As I mentioned, there are several strategies available, but the one I want to share now is the Roth IRA conversion. A Roth IRA conversion is one of the more popular methods people use to convert their Tax-Deferred accounts to Tax-Free accounts. With a Roth IRA, you pay the tax on the deposit, and you receive growth tax-free. That means income-tax-free for you and tax-free for your heirs. Keep in mind that you want to review your tax-deferred assets and develop a strategy that works for you and your situation rather than just choosing the most common strategy without doing your research."

"Of course," Jenny acknowledged.

"Also, there's more to it than just the investment vehicle you use," the Architect continued. "Knowing about Roth IRAs is important, but that's not the whole picture. It's also about knowing when to start moving your money out of your IRAs or 401(k)s, and what dollar amount not to exceed. Living Tax-Free is like healthy living; it's not a crash diet, it's a mindset, a lifestyle. It's all about how you set up your investments, how you design your income plan, what deductions are available to you, and so much more.

"Now, a word of caution. Roth IRA conversions are taxed. You will have to pay taxes on the amount converted in the year of the conversion. However, paying the tax from the same account you are converting would be subject to an IRS penalty if done before age 59½. That's why I recommend paying the taxes from assets outside of the original IRA instead.

"Yikes! If it's that complicated, why do it at all?" Robert asked.

"Great question," began the Architect. "It's true that the taxes you'll pay on the conversion could lower your current retirement savings. But what do we expect tax rates to look like in the future? If we believe they'll go up, then any likelihood of higher future tax rates can make a Roth IRA conversion a strategy worth considering."

"I see," Robert said. "Thank you."

"I also recommend consulting with a qualified tax advisor when considering a Roth conversion since the conversion of a traditional IRA or other qualified assets could impact your personal tax situation. The conversion could require additional tax withholding or estimated tax payments, potentially resulting in the loss of certain tax deductions or credits.

"We're going to want to be up close and personal for this next build," the Architect said, leading them back into their Financial House. The Architect smiled as a mild shake rolled through the structure. The couple looked upwards as three thick support beams appeared. They gazed around at the house they were nearly finished designing.

Summary

- Designing your Financial House with tax efficiency in mind can make your retirement plan more successful.
- There are three types of investment taxations— Taxable, Tax-Deferred, and Tax-Free.
- At age seventy-two, you must begin withdrawing your IRA money as income. These RMDs (Required Minimum Distributions) are required whether you need the money as income or not.
- When you invest in an IRA, you are agreeing to an arrangement with the IRS that gives them control over when you are allowed and required to withdraw your money, and how much money you must withdraw.
- You can strategically reduce the tax you pay on the money in your IRA, 401(k), TSA, and other similar accounts. It's important to learn all the options available to you and discover which strategy works best for you.

Questions to Consider

1. Do you have money in IRAs, 401(k)s, or Thrift Savings Plans? Are you aware that you must begin withdrawing RMDs (Required Minimum Distributions) from these accounts beginning at age seventy-two?

____

____

____

2. Do you have a strategy to take back control of the money in your IRA or similar accounts?

____

____

____

Notes

PART VI

THE ROOF

Chapter Twelve

RISK AND YOUR INVESTMENTS

"We're almost finished constructing your Financial House," the Architect revealed excitedly, leading them back to their drafting table to sit. "The last step is building your Roof. The Roof represents your risk investments. There are two ways to build your Roof. I'll mention the first one briefly, just so you understand its relation to the second method. The first way is Passive Investing."

"Passive Investing?" Jenny asked. "I've never heard of that."

"Actually, you may have heard of it," the Architect said. "Have you heard of the Buy-and-Hold strategy? This method simply follows the market. It means you're just along for the ride. You experience all the ups and all the downs. Like a roller coaster following the track, your money follows the market."

"Okay," Robert said. "Isn't that just part of investing in the stock market? I always thought that's how all market investing worked."

"For the Buy-and-Hold strategy, you're right," the Architect said, "but it's not the only way. Most people take the Passive Investing approach. Sure, there have been losses, but most investments in the market so far have bounced back and made up those losses only to keep growing. Of course, the past is no guarantee of future results, but that pattern of growth has been consistent throughout the history of the stock market."

"I think I understand," Jenny said. "You're saying we can just buy shares and hold our money in the market so long as our Foundation, Walls, and Beams are in place?"

"I'm saying that's one opportunity," the Architect confirmed. "While Passive Investing can potentially be ideal for someone investing in their twenties, thirties, or even forties, it tends to become less ideal the older we get, or rather, the closer we get to retirement."

"Why is it less ideal?" Robert asked.

"Because the older we get," the Architect explained, "the less time we have available to make up for any potential losses. We discussed how paper losses become real losses when we start using our investments as income. Your Foundation, Walls, and Beams secure your income needs without risking that income. Your Roof construction focuses more on growth. However, while investing in your Roof won't necessarily hurt your lifestyle, it doesn't mean you want to take unnecessary risks with your investments, as this money has the potential to greatly increase your lifestyle."

"That makes sense," Jenny said. "So, Passive Investing may not be the method for us as we close in on our retirement. What's the other option?"

"The other option," the Architect said, "as you might guess, is called Active Investing."

"Is that like day trading?" Robert asked. "Because I'll be honest with you, if that's the other option, I'd rather stick with Passive Investing than be glued to a computer for the rest of my life. I'll take a modest lifestyle with no stress over the anxiety of checking the market every morning and evening. How could you enjoy your retirement years like that?"

"Oh boy, you're not kidding," the Architect said, shaking his head. "That doesn't sound like much fun to me either. Fortunately, Active Investing has other strategies from which to choose. Regardless of which method you've used up to this point, I'm sure you've had the help of financial professionals along the way—stockbrokers or financial advisors, for example."

"Sure," Jenny said. "Someone who understands things better than we do."

"Well, if your financial professional is doing their job right," the Architect continued, "then they are watching the markets and the economy so they can inform you when it's time to pull out of certain investments, or when to jump into others. Guess what? That's Active Investing. Now, what if you could have a team of wealth managers studying the market and working hard to reduce the risk you're taking with your investments?"

"Sounds great to me," Jenny said.

"Of course," the Architect continued, "a lot of planning goes into Active Investing. First, I'd want to sit down with both of you to analyze the risk you're currently taking and compare that to your risk comfort level."

"Our comfort level?" Rob asked.

"In other words, how much you could afford to lose before you'd start to feel uncomfortable," the Architect replied. "Believe it or not, a lot of people are taking more risk with their investments than they think they are. Once I've pointed that out to them, they want to make corrections. My team of wealth managers and I generally use three models—Moderate Investing, Growth Investing, and Focus Investing."

"Now, wait a minute," Robert said, a bit nervous. "So, you start with Moderate? What happened to Conservative?"

"We've already covered Conservative," the Architect said. "That investment level is what we used to build your Walls. That's precisely why we don't start building your Financial House with the Roof." The Architect pulled a folder from the papers on the drafting table. He fanned out several pictures of Alice in Wonderland proportioned houses. "Remember these photos of very oddly constructed financial houses?" These investors either overbuilt towering walls with tiny, insufficient roofs, or they overbuilt gigantic roofs on overly modest walls that can't hold them up. Golly, some of these are even missing pieces of their basic foundations," he added, gesturing to a photo of a house sinking into the earth on one side. "Just like building a real house, you make sure your Foundation and Walls are exactly as you want them before you even begin working on your roof. That's why we start our Roof investments with Moderate Investments."

"Okay," Robert said. "I'm on board."

"So, let's start with Moderate," the Architect said. "Moderate Investing is a portfolio that consists of about 65 percent in stocks or equities and around 35 percent in fixed income, such as bonds. This step is for investors who are more conservative with their investments but still eager for the kind of growth that can come from investing in the market. In the Moderate model, our managers aim to keep your losses no higher than 12 percent to 15 percent. Of course, no one can guarantee market performance, but that's the goal."

"Right," Jenny said.

"Second, let's talk about Growth," the Architect continued. "Growth Investing is a portfolio consisting of 85 percent in stocks or equities and 15 percent in bonds. If you're willing to take a little more risk to take advantage of a little more potential on the upside, this method is for you. In this model, our managers aim to lose no more than 15 percent to 20 percent."

"I'm following you so far," Jenny said.

"Our third and final level is Focus Investment. Like the name suggests, this is for investors primarily *focused* on the potential for growth. This means you're 100 percent invested in stocks and equities. In other words, when the market's down, you're down. When the market's up, you're up. Even within the Focus Portfolio, it's important not to slip into Passive Investing. That's why my team of Wealth Managers is working hard to keep your losses no more than 20 percent to 25 percent under this model. For example, in 2008, when the market was down over 38 percent, our managers' goal was to lose no more than 20 percent to 25 percent. So, even in our Focus model, your risk level can be less than those who simply use the Buy-and-Hold strategy."

"I understand," Robert said.

"And that," the Architect said, "is our Roof. Now, before we move on, I want to discuss what this means for your risk level. Let's imagine you've chosen to invest under the Focus model, and you come across a bad year for the market. For example, let's imagine you lose that 25 percent. Have you actually lost 25 percent of your total assets? No! Thanks to your Walls, you have investments that are not at risk. So, if you invest half of your investable assets into your Walls and the other half into the Roof, you've averaged a loss of only 12.5 percent overall. When you take both the Walls and the

Roof into account, that shows you the total risk you're taking overall."

"Wow," Jenny said. "I can't believe how much we've learned. I can really see the advantage of having our investments divided between the Walls and the Roof."

"That's right," the Architect said. "Investing this way can really help alleviate the downside."

"I would definitely sleep better at night, knowing we're invested strategically," Robert said.

"Great," the Architect said. "There are a few final things I'd like to mention pertaining to your Roof. These most recent years have been quite a ride for investors, so let's talk about Wealth Insurance."

"Wealth insurance?" Robert asked. "That sounds made up."

"Quite the contrary," the Architect said. "Wealth Insurance is what many financial experts are calling investing in gold and silver coins."

"Oh, I've heard a little bit about that," Jenny said.

"Now," the Architect said matter-of-factly, "I want to say that while all financial needs and situations are unique, it's important to understand how and why at least a little gold and silver fit into most portfolios."

"Okay," Jenny said.

"If you choose to invest in gold or silver, I recommend investing in non-qualified coins rather than qualified coins."

"What's the difference between qualified and non-qualified?" Robert asked.

"Well," the Architect began, "for starters, non-qualified gold and silver is the only investment that you can hold in your hands. Qualified coins are usually held for you by a custodian because those coins generally get invested in IRA and Roth IRA investments. I recommend being able to hold your own coins."

"And how much do you recommend we invest in gold and silver?" Jenny asked.

"Every situation is different, so I'd make recommendations based on an individual's financial circumstances," the Architect replied. "That said, I think a general starting point is 5 to 10 percent. I certainly wouldn't recommend exceeding 15 percent in most cases."

"Okay," Robert said, "having something like that on hand makes sense. Let me ask you, though, why do you call it Wealth Insurance?"

"That's a great question," the Architect said. "Gold and silver have the potential to offset market losses and inflation."

"Makes sense," Jenny said.

"And you can tuck that gold and silver away safely," the Architect said, looking over the blueprint he'd sketched for the couple, "right there."

He took his pencil and sketched a little treasure chest in the attic. Robert and Jenny laughed.

"Now," the Architect said, "I'd like to talk about real estate."

"Great," Robert said. "I was just going to ask you about this. We have a little investment property we bought some time ago. We used it every summer as a vacation home, and we'd rent it out in between visits. Now that our kids are all grown up and have families of their own, we don't use it nearly as often, so we started to rent it out full-time. The problem is the maintenance and the upkeep are practically a job on their own. I'd hate to retire and still have these responsibilities on the side. What's the best way to handle that?"

"That's a great question," the Architect said. "Rental properties inevitably come with maintenance and upkeep, or as I like to call it, the three T's: tenants, trash, and toilets."

"That's exactly right," Robert said, laughing. "That sums up all the stuff I'm sick of right there."

"When you're tired of being a landlord," the Architect continued, "you can liquidate the real estate by doing a 1031 Exchange and investing in real estate property through a statutory trust or real estate funds that serve as high-quality cash-flow properties. You'd still be getting rental cash flow that could potentially be mostly tax-free without the added headache of managing the property yourselves. Many people like getting the income from their rental properties without the associated responsibilities."

"That sounds great," Jenny said, nudging her husband. "We should look into that."

The Architect deftly sketched the roof on their blueprint and motioned for Robert and Jenny to step back from the construction site so they could take in the full view. The ground shook precariously, and a lovely roof appeared on the house. A sudden gust of wind accompanied the settling of the roof, causing the couple to shield their eyes from the swirling dust. When they looked back, the house was no longer a bare bones structure, but a fully finished home, complete with windows, doors, landscaping, and a fresh coat of paint. Jenny gasped in delight.

"There it is," the Architect said, proudly, "**Your Financial House, Custom Designed**™ to fit your needs."

"Thank you for all you've done," Robert said. "I feel like we know what to do now. With the proper planning, some hard work, and a little help from our Architect, we may be celebrating our own retirement party soon."

"Always happy to help," the Architect said, genuinely pleased.

Summary

- There are two strategies for investing in the stock market—Passive Investing and Active Investing.
- Passive Investing is better known as the Buy-and-Hold Strategy in which your money rides the waves of the market.
- Active Investing with a team of wealth managers allows you to take only the risk you're comfortable with through three levels:
    - Moderate (Portfolio: 65 percent in stocks, 35 percent in bonds)
    - Growth (Portfolio: 85 percent in stocks, 15 percent in bonds)
    - Focus (Portfolio: 100 percent in stocks)
- Investing in gold and silver coins as "Wealth Insurance" gives you a physical investment that can offset stock market losses and help keep pace with inflation.
- If you have invested in real estate property, you can reinvest in a real estate fund or real property through a statutory trust that offers primarily tax-free, high-quality cash flow without the added headache of serving as landlord.

Questions to Consider

1. Are you passively invested in the market, using the Buy-and-Hold method, or actively invested in the market, using a team of wealth managers?

____

____

2. What is your risk comfort level? What percentage of your invested assets would you feel comfortable losing?

____

____

3. Have you invested in gold and/or silver coins as a piece of your investment portfolio? If not, have you considered how gold and/or silver could potentially serve as "Wealth Insurance"?

____

____

4. Are you tired of dealing with the three T's: tenants, trash, and toilets of any current rental properties? If so, have you considered ways to continue receiving mostly tax-free income while avoiding the headache of being a landlord?

____

____

____

Notes

PART VII

THE FINANCIAL HOUSE

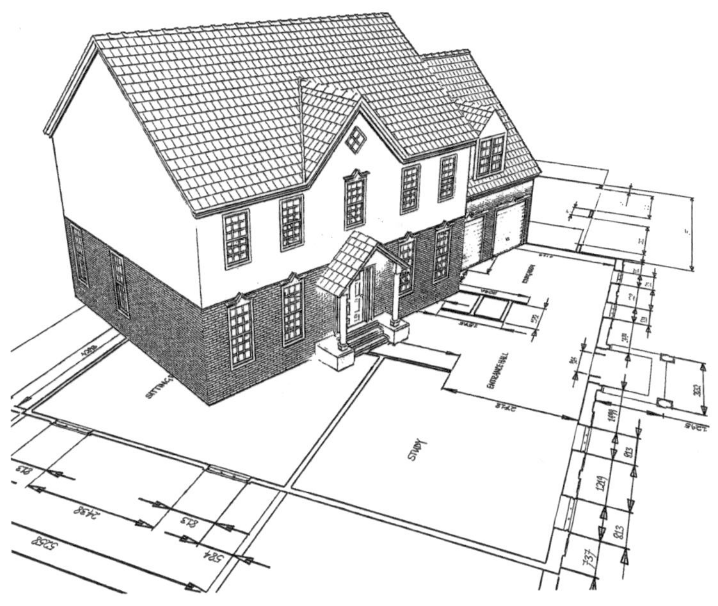

Chapter Thirteen

CUSTOM DESIGNED

The couple stood in silence, staring up at their beautiful Financial House. The Architect led them back to the drafting table to show them a completely detailed version of their house blueprints. "I think you'll find this finished product quite to your liking as well," he remarked. Jenny and Robert took a closer look. Notes, numbers, and arrows signifying their own investments, accounts, and financial needs covered the page. These numbers and accounts served as measurements for their Cornerstones, their Foundation, their Walls, the Support Beams, and eventually their Roof. The design was astounding.

"It's better than I could have imagined," Robert said.

"It's beautiful," Jenny said, her eyes beginning to water. "How can we ever thank you?"

"You are quite welcome, my friends," the Architect replied. "I want you to remember that this is your blueprint plan only. Building your Financial House may vary based on things that come up during the construction."

"We'll remember," Robert said.

"Also," the Architect continued, "just like a real house, your Financial House requires regular maintenance and upkeep. Your priorities could change, meaning that your Financial House may require renovations or upgrades."

"Can we count on you to help us through those processes as well?" Jenny asked hopefully.

"Of course you can," the Architect said, smiling. He picked up the blueprint and handed it to the couple to examine it more thoroughly.

"Look," Robert said, pointing at the blueprint, "the first Cornerstone has between three to twelve months' income set aside in our Cash Reserves."

"And there's the Healthcare Cornerstone," Jenny added, placing her finger on the paper. "With the right healthcare decisions, long-term-care coverage, and life insurance, I'm more confident we'll be okay no matter what happens."

"Our kids will appreciate the hard work we put into our Pre-planning and Legacy Preparation Cornerstone," Robert replied. "Our documents will all be in order, and our funeral expenses covered."

"And our house and car will be covered with the proper insurance coverage with this Cornerstone," Jenny said.

"With a little extra on top," Robert said, smiling, "thanks to that Umbrella policy."

"And there's our foundation," Jenny said, breathing a sigh of relief. "We've worried for so many years that we wouldn't have enough to retire if something were to happen? Now we know our foundation is solid, providing us with an income plan we can't outlive, so we know our basic needs will be covered no matter what."

"Of course," Robert said, "and on top of that Foundation, we have strong Walls. Walls that will help us enjoy our lifestyle as well as help us keep up with inflation."

"Don't forget the Beams!" Jenny said, pointing and rubbing her finger along the lines. "Knowing our investments are tax-efficient and mostly tax-free helps me know our Financial House is properly supported."

"And last, but certainly not least," Robert said, "our Roof. With the rest of our Financial House so stable, I believe we can take more investment risk than we'd previously thought was safe. Who knows?! Maybe we'll find the next Apple to invest in. Or Amazon."

"Wouldn't that be nice," Jenny said, leaning her head on her husband's shoulder. "We've been worried for so long. It's amazing to have that burden lifted."

The Architect took a quick glance at his watch. "Well, I'll be! We really ought to be getting back to the office!"

"Oh yes, I almost forgot!" Jenny added laughing. The sun was already casting long shadows.

With a snap of his fingers, the Architect dissolved their surroundings while Jenny and Robert gazed at their Financial House until it vanished. They found themselves standing in the familiar, cozy office where they had started the day.

Robert shook his head to get reoriented and turned his attention to the Architect. "Thank you for all your help."

"You're very welcome," the Architect said, shaking Robert's hand. He extended his hand to Jenny as well, but she went in for a hug instead.

"A handshake isn't enough for all you've done," she said, smiling at him. "Thank you again."

Robert rolled up the blueprint, grabbed Jenny's hand, and started moving quickly toward the door.

"Where are you off to in such a hurry?" the Architect asked.

"We've got to get home," Robert said. "I've got a retirement barbecue to plan. We'll need ribs and burgers, and we've got to see if Tom and Lisa have plans for next weekend. There's so much to do."

"You're invited too, of course," Jenny shouted back excitedly as her husband practically dragged her from the office in his rush.

"I wouldn't miss it for the world, you two," the Architect said, waving at them.

When Robert reached the car, he opened the door for his wife and hurried around to his side. He held her hand and looked at her with a soft smile.

They both knew the real adventure was about to begin.

YOUR NEXT STEP: MOVING IN

The information you've just read in this book serves as a blueprint to *Your Financial House, Custom Designed*™, but you can't live in a blueprint.

To turn this blueprint into your very own Financial House, the next step you should take is to reach out to the Financial Architects at Eric Scott Financial. Our team can review your unique situation to help you determine the best way to design and build the retirement of your dreams.

Contact Us

Office: (435)773-9444
Email: info@ericscottfinancial.com

ERIC L. SCOTT

Eric L. Scott is the president and founder of Eric Scott Financial. Eric began his career in the financial and insurance industry in 1983. He set out on his own in 1987 with a keen desire to help people more completely. He loves to visit with people and really get to know them. His goal is to help more people reach their retirement goals.

Equipped with the knowledge from over thirty-five years of experience, Eric shares his vast financial knowledge throughout St. George and its surrounding communities. He offers community education classes on various financial and retirement topics. He also previously hosted a financial radio program called *Financial Crossroads*. He currently records a podcast, *Financial House Design,* with his co-host and fellow advisor, Katie Prosser.

Eric has previously published three books, *The Five Crossroads* (2012), *Shattering IRA Misconceptions* (2015), and *The Three Pillars* (2022). With these books, Eric approaches tough financial and retirement questions using a unique storytelling format that allows readers to follow along the retirement journey of a fictional couple as they explore their financial concerns.

Eric loves spending time with his family and serving his church and community. He and his wife have been married since 1979 and live in Saint George. They enjoy spending time with their children and grandchildren and spend much of their leisure time traveling so they can enjoy all the beauty this nation has to offer.

PAUL SCOTT

Paul Scott is the content manager and copywriter at Eric Scott Financial. He's been writing since he could pick up a pencil, his interest evolving from hobby to passion over the years. He joined the Eric Scott Financial Team in 2009.

Paul is responsible for creating email newsletters and blog articles, curating social media content as well as writing scripts for the team's financial podcast, *Financial House Design*, and previously the radio program, *Financial Crossroads*. While Paul generally tends to be "the man behind the curtain," you may also have heard him on occasion in the radio program's earlier episodes.

In 2011, Paul and Eric sat down to begin writing a financial advice book. Armed with Paul's background in fiction and Eric's financial expertise, they were able to create a unique storytelling experience that both entertained and educated the reader about the importance of financial planning. That book was *The Five Crossroads* (2012).

When he's not writing, Paul can often be found with his nose buried in a book, perusing the exhibits at a local museum, or taking a walk around the block. As a widowed father, he spends most of his time with his beautiful daughter.

KATIE PROSSER

Since joining Eric Scott Financial in 2011, Katie has distinguished herself as a dedicated and insightful advisor. Her commitment to crafting tailored financial plans allows those she works with to enter retirement with confidence. As a critical part of the team, Katie excels in providing exceptional service, ensuring that each client's unique needs are met. Her expertise as an Investment Advisor Representative with licenses in Life and Health Insurance, and a comprehensive knowledge of Medicare, makes her an invaluable member of our team.

Raised in Northern Utah, Katie has been a proud resident of St. George since 2004. Alongside her husband, she is currently raising three beautiful children. When not helping people plan for their retirement, Katie enjoys several hobbies. Her passions include yoga, hiking, reading, and spending time with her family.

Meet the Team

ABOUT ERIC SCOTT FINANCIAL

Eric Scott Financial is a financial service firm headquartered in St. George, Utah. The diligent team members have dedicated their service to educating and guiding their clients down the path to retirement while striving to achieve their financial goals and help them enjoy their retirement dreams.

The firm's foundation is rooted in core values that we believe have enabled Eric Scott Financial to become a pillar for financial advice in the community. Those strong core values include communication, education, and service.

We take pride in teaching and distributing information in an easy-to-understand way. Our goal is to have our clients leave our office with confidence and pride in their ability to succeed, *not* exit with a stack of convoluted paperwork and confusing financial jargon.

Our team at Eric Scott Financial believes in building a relationship through service, not numbers. We want clients to feel comfortable with them.

If you have financial questions, concerns, or would like to learn more about how to lay out the plans for your own *Financial House*, call Eric Scott Financial at (435) 773-9444.

Notes

ERIC SCOTT FINANCIAL

OUR STORY

"We take care of our audience every night because they take care of us. It's the only guarantee that you'll ever get. That's why we never phone it in. You never know who's out there in the audience. Someone might be seeing you for the first time." – Bruce Springsteen, Rolling Stone Magazine, 1986

Now, I may not be as rock 'n' roll as The Boss, but I share his philosophy. I know that every person who walks through our doors has a unique story and a different set of goals, concerns, and aspirations. That's why I make it my mission to treat each person with the same excitement and enthusiasm as I did my first meeting. I know that retirement planning can be a daunting and overwhelming process, but retirement should be a memorable experience.

My mother and father instilled two values that I carry with me every day – hard work and service. I have a passion for helping people achieve financial security and peace of mind. One of my greatest joys is when I see the relief in my clients' eyes as they say, "I'm going to be okay." That's because I know those simple words represent so much more than just financial security. They're a symbol of hope, of a brighter future, and of the freedom to live the retirement lifestyle they've worked so hard for.

The team at Eric Scott Financial shares these values with me. We understand that our clients are entrusting us with their future, and we take that responsibility seriously. Our approach to financial and retirement planning is different from the rest for that reason. We want people to understand that it's about so much more than just the numbers. That's why we created our retirement planning process, Your Financial House, Custom Designed. It's about helping people plan for the unexpected, preparing for the worst-case scenario, while allowing them to give themselves permission to make their retirement dreams a reality.

We wrote this book to share *The Financial House* with people just like you. We want you to realize that retirement planning isn't just about whether you have enough money to last the rest of your life. It's about so much more. This book is for everyone who wants to take control of their future and design a blueprint for the life they want in retirement. The book is designed to reflect your values and a deep understanding of your retirement goals.

Through our work at Eric Scott Financial, my team and I have helped people overcome their worries and anxieties around money. We empower our clients to take charge of their financial future, no matter what challenges might come their way. And in doing so, enjoy a retirement, and a life well-lived.

Sincerely,
Eric L. Scott